Wrinkled Deep in Time

Wrinkled Deep in Time

AGING IN SHAKESPEARE MAURICE CHARNEY

COLUMBIA UNIVERSITY PRESS ♚ NEW YORK

Columbia University Press
Publishers Since 1893
New York   Chichester, West Sussex

Library of Congress Cataloging-in-Publication Data
Charney, Maurice.
Wrinkled deep in time : aging in Shakespeare / Maurice Charney.
p.   cm.
Includes bibliographical references and index.
ISBN 978-0-231-14230-4 (cloth : acid-free paper)
1. Shakespeare, William, 1564-1616—Criticism and interpretation.
2. Aging in literature.   3. Old age in literature.   I. Title.
PR3069.A38C53   2009
822.3'3—dc22   2008053440

Columbia University Press books are printed on permanent and durable acid-free paper.
This book was printed on paper with recycled content.
Printed in the United States of America
c 10 9 8 7 6 5 4 3 2 1

References to Internet Web sites (URLs) were accurate at the time of writing. Neither the author nor Columbia University Press is responsible for URLs that may have expired or changed since the manuscript was prepared.

For Bobbie

My Muse of Eighty-sixth Street

CONTENTS

ACKNOWLEDGMENTS

Although I have benefited tremendously from reading the notes to various editions, especially the Arden and Signet editions, I have also learned a lot about Shakespeare from animated conversations with scholars and students alike. I have gleaned much wisdom from attending the Shakespeare Seminar of Columbia University. I am grateful to Naomi Liebler for information about the seminar "Shakespeare's Geezers" presented at the Shakespeare Association of America meetings in Philadelphia in 2006, which I was not able to attend. The following participants kindly forwarded their papers, from which I have greatly profited: Alberto Cacicedo, Anthony Ellis, Dorothea Kehler, Mary Ellen Lamb, and Richard Levin. Thanks to Jim Shapiro for sharing his ideas about aging in Shakespeare. I appreciate the painstaking and intelligent reading of the manuscript by Jim Bednarz and the creative copyediting of Henry Krawitz.

N.B.: I have kept notes to a minimum in the belief that they should be restricted to issues related to aging in Shakespeare rather than to general topics about style, character, and staging.

Wrinkled Deep in Time

INTRODUCTION

There is a certain autobiographical element in this project. In the past I have written on Shakespeare's Roman plays (especially the presentational imagery), two books on the style and fictionality of *Hamlet*, a study of *Titus Andronicus*, a comprehensive account of all of Shakespeare, and an investigation of love and lust in Shakespeare. Yet I have never dared to broach the formidable topic of aging in Shakespeare. However, now that I am approaching Lear's age, I am embarking on a study that fills me with trepidation. My perspective has changed considerably from my undergraduate years at Harvard, when I devoured the notes in the sixteen plays that George Lyman Kittredge closely annotated, and when I was thrilled by Maurice Schwartz's rendition of King Lear in Yiddish at the theater on Second Avenue in New York, which elicited copious weeping from the audience.

It seems to me now that Shakespeare was preoccupied with issues of aging that must have had an acute relation to his own sense of growing old. Many of the old men and women in Shakespeare's works are foolish in their intemperance and in their claim not to have changed from what they were in the past—in other words, in their refusal to acknowledge the ravages of time. Some are reverting to second childhood, like King Lear, or senility, like Polonius. But there is also a positive sense that with the accumulation of experience comes wisdom and fortitude. Falstaff is a type of ideal figure who tries to maintain the illusion of a youthful old age, at least in the *Henry IV* plays. And Duke Senior and Old Adam in *As You Like It* approach a pastoral ideal of the Golden Age. Although the time when old age sets in may differ in the twenty-first century from the early onset of old age in Shakespeare's lifetime, the infirmities remain pretty much the same as they were four hundred years ago.

Jaques's "Seven Ages of Man" speech in *As You Like It* (2.7.139–66) is a fairly standard set piece. Seven is a common division, although the number could vary according to the seasons, the astrological signs, the hours, and so forth. The ages of man were often represented graphically. Jaques's speech is unusually satiric and dismissive in tone, as if no age is the right one. Old age seems to begin with "the lean and slippered pantaloon," the Pantalone character from the Italian commedia dell'arte,

> With spectacles on nose and pouch on side;
> His youthful hose, well saved, a world too wide
> For his shrunk shank, and his big manly voice,
> Turning again toward childish treble, pipes
> And whistles in his [its] sound. (159–63)[1]

This is the enfeebled old man, like Polonius in *Hamlet* and Nestor in *Troilus and Cressida*. The seventh age, representing total decrepitude,

> Is second childishness and mere [total] oblivion,
> Sans teeth, sans eyes, sans taste, sans everything. (165–66)

The French *sans*, meaning "without," is part of Jaques's affected style, effectively mocked by Rosaline in *Love's Labor's Lost* when Berowne uses the word in his apology: "Sans *sans*, I pray you" (5.2.417).

The ages of man theme[2] also appears in the song Feste sings at the end of *Twelfth Night*:

> When that I was and a little tiny boy
> > With hey, ho, the wind and the rain,
> A foolish thing was but a toy [trifle],
> > For the rain it raineth every day. (5.1.391–94)

The wind and the rain indicate the inevitable passage of time, specifically time the destroyer, as in the *Sonnets*. The next to last stanza of Feste's song evokes a melancholy old age similar to that of Jaques:

> But when I came unto my beds,
> > With hey, ho, the wind and the rain,
> With tosspots [drunkards] still had drunken heads,
> > For the rain it raineth every day. (403–6)

The drunkenness is a sign of despair as the Clown nears death.

The last stanza posits an endless progression of time since the world began. It serves the standard function of an epilogue to appeal to the audience for applause:

> A great while ago the world begun,
> > Hey, ho, the wind and the rain;
> But that's all one, our play is done,
> > And we'll strive to please you every day. (407–10)

It is interesting that Feste's song from *Twelfth Night* is adapted by the Fool in *King Lear*, occurring just before the king enters the hovel on the "blasted heath":

> He that has and a little tiny wit,
> With heigh-ho, the wind and the rain,
> Must make content with his fortunes fit,
> Though the rain it raineth every day. (3.2.74–77)

The wind and the rain represent the adversities of time as it wears everything down. The old man in Shakespeare is a victim of the wind and the rain in this metaphorical sense.

How old is old in Shakespeare? Cleopatra, who is clearly not old by contemporary standards, says that she is "with Phoebus' amorous pinches black / And wrinkled deep in time" (*Antony and Cleopatra*, 1.5.28–29). The historical Cleopatra was married to Antony in 36 B.C. and died in 30 B.C., aged thirty-nine.[3] Shakespeare makes no reference to these dates, but in the play Cleopatra is thought to be in her late thirties—hardly old in the twenty-first century—although she was nearing the end of her child-bearing years, which was one of the markers of old age for a woman in Shakespeare's time.

In the *Sonnets* the ravages of time surprisingly appear in both the poet and his love when they are at most middle-aged to our way of thinking. For example, Sonnet 2 opens with a surprising quatrain:

> When forty winters shall besiege thy brow,
> And dig deep trenches in thy beauty's field,
> Thy youth's proud livery, so gazed on now,
> Will be a tottered weed of small worth held.

That the youth's beauty will be transformed at forty into a tattered garment of little value comes as a surprise to us, but forty is already well on the way to fifty, the conventional year for the onset of old age in men in Shakespeare's time.

Although there is a great deal of gerontological data about England in Shakespeare's time, it is mixed and unsystematic.[4] Parish registers are complete and accurate for some places and extremely sparse for others. We know certain general facts, for example, that infant mortality was extremely high and that childhood mortality before the age of 21 was also high. According to Peter Laslett's calculations, life expectancy from birth in 1601 was 38.12 years.[5] However, according to Lawrence Stone's figures, if you managed to live until you were 15, then life expectancy increased to 54.28 years for men.[6] It was much lower for women (about

45–50).[7] Of course, there were many older persons in the court and in government service. Presumably they had access to much more nutritious food and better medical services. For the same reasons those connected with the church lived much longer than the general population. Life expectancy was clearly related to class and income—as it still is today.

Shakespeare generally doesn't mention specific ages. Prospero in *The Tempest* is in his mid-forties, as is Leontes in *The Winter's Tale*, but they are both represented as old men. It is curious that in *Romeo and Juliet* Lady Capulet seems to be about twenty-eight, but at the end of the play she says:

O me, this sight of death is as a bell
That warns my old age to a sepulcher. (5.3.206–7)

Her "old age" is contextual and is connected with her extreme grief over her daughter Juliet's death. Similarly, Macbeth and Lady Macbeth seem to grow old in the course of the play.

The issue of old age is somewhat different for women since it is closely connected with the onset of menopause.[8] Women past their child-bearing years were regarded as old, a belief connected with the notion that women's beauty fades quickly following menopause. The general feeling was that a woman aged forty or forty-five was an old lady—or at least rapidly aging—whereas men were not considered old until about ten years later. It's not so surprising that Cleopatra thinks of herself as "wrinkled deep in time" (1.5.29). Shakespeare makes no mention of her age except to say that "age cannot wither her" (2.2.241), but the historical Cleopatra was in her late thirties. In the closet scene Hamlet is preoccupied with his mother's sexuality. Despite his conflicting and contradictory notions, he is genuinely surprised that his mother should exude strong desire:

for at your age
The heyday in the blood is tame, it's humble,
And waits upon the judgment. (3.4.69–71)

In Renaissance physiology the blood was thought to carry sexual impulses. Although Hamlet identifies his mother as menopausal, no specific age is ever provided.

This book concentrates on Shakespeare's text rather than the literature on aging in Shakespeare's time, a subject more than adequately treated by other commentators.[9] Chapter 1 presents the most important representation of aging in Shakespeare, namely, *King Lear*. The old king, aged fourscore and upward, presents both negative and positive aspects of aging. He is impulsive and imperious. The testing of his daughters at the beginning of the play serves as the catalyst for his own tragedy. Yet in his madness he comes to a new understanding of himself and the reality that surrounds him. Many of the crucial points about old age are echoed in the figures of Gloucester and Kent. *Titus Andronicus*, an early tragedy, presents many of the issues about old age that will be developed later in *King Lear*. The king in *Cymbeline* is very like King Lear, although he is not much developed in this late romance.

Chapter 2 explores the process of growing old in Shakespeare. There is obviously a difference between the amount of time that elapses in a concentrated scene and the amount of time that is thought to be passing in the entire narrative, often called double time or long and short time. Characters seem to age in relation to dire events occurring in the play. For example, Juliet seems considerably older when she drinks Friar Lawrence's potion than she was earlier in the play, where she is identified as a girl not yet fourteen. This is also true of Hamlet, Richard II, and Timon: they all seem to grow older toward the ends of their plays, as if age is determined psychologically and in relation to the dramatic context. This phenomenon is most remarkable in *Macbeth*, where both Macbeth and Lady Macbeth end the play as old and despairing individuals. Macbeth's way of life "is fall'n into the sear, the yellow leaf" (5.3.23).

Chapter 3 deals with images of Time the Destroyer, especially in the *Sonnets*. Shakespeare uses traditional attributes of Time, such as the scythe and the hourglass, to establish the relentless and inevitable course of growing old and eventually dying. Writing poetry and procreating are ways of defying time. The *Sonnets* are preoccupied with the destruction of beauty, vividly expressed in the image of wrinkles and also of white hair. There are three much-repeated images to convey the ravages of time: trees losing their leaves in winter, the light fading in a natural day, and fire consuming itself and producing ashes. Shakespeare was only in his thirties when most of the sonnets were written, but the sense of relentless aging fits in well with the imagery of the plays.

Chapter 4 deals with "heavy" or hard fathers, a character type developed from the *senex*, or old man, a stock figure from Roman comedy, and Plautus in particular. Shakespeare's hard fathers are very patriarchal and controlling, especially in relation to their marriageable daughters. The best example is Prospero in *The Tempest*, a magician who arranges his daughter Miranda's marriage to Ferdinand. Capulet's rage against his daughter Juliet in *Romeo and Juliet* because she refuses to marry Paris is another notable example. Egeus in *A Midsummer Night's Dream* and Brabantio in *Othello* also vigorously object to their daughters' marriage choices. To this list one could add Shylock in *The Merchant of Venice* and his relation to his daughter Jessica. Northumberland in the English history plays is a hard father in terms of his abandonment of his son Hotspur in battle.

Chapter 5 continues the *senex* theme of the previous chapter. Polonius, Nestor, and Menenius are counselors of state, skillful in rhetoric—and long-winded. There is a striking moment in *Hamlet* when Polonius loses the thread of his discourse and has to reconnect with what he was just saying. He is a masterful orator, but his flamboyant speech is so excessive that the queen has to remind him: "More matter, with less art" (2.2.95). Nestor in *Troilus and Cressida* is a much-respected ancient figure from the *Iliad*, yet he is also ambiguous in the sense that it is not at all clear whether he is to be considered wise or superannuated. Menenius in *Coriolanus* is an effective politician who represents aristocratic values. His witty fable of the Belly and the Members, drawn from the commonplaces of Renaissance political theory, mainly serves to pacify the plebeians and their tribunes. It is persuasive yet also specious.

Chapter 6 is concerned with wise old men. In particular, it focuses on *As You Like It* and the characters of Duke Senior, Old Adam, and the aged shepherd Corin. All are highly idealized, pastoral figures reminiscent of a kind of Golden Age. This is also true of Gonzalo in *The Tempest*, whose ideal commonwealth is an original, heterodox utopia. Another group of characters in Shakespeare achieve wisdom right before dying and are transformed by meditative, philosophical speculations. This is certainly true of both Henry IV in *2 Henry IV* and Richard II. In *The Merchant of Venice* Portia's dead father rules beneficently with respect to her marriage choice through the folklore device of the three caskets.

Chapter 7 is devoted to Falstaff, who represents the Renaissance ideal of the young old man. We see a great deal of his verbal dexterity and his acting skill. As a lover he is adulated by Dame Quickly and Doll Tearsheet. The warm emotional tone of the *Henry IV* plays is abruptly disrupted by Prince Hal's—now King Henry V's—rejection of Falstaff. He is quite a different character in *The Merry Wives of Windsor*, Shakespeare's only attempt at a city comedy. Here he is no longer the young old man but an aging mock-lover against whom the Windsor wives take their revenge. In *2 Henry IV* Justice Shallow is developed as a countertype to—almost a parody of—Falstaff, as is the figure of Justice Silence.

Chapter 8 focuses on Othello and Leontes. They are both old men—especially Leontes following the sixteen-year gap in the middle of *The Winter's Tale*. Othello bears some surprising resemblances to the *pantalone*, or old man, of the commedia dell'arte, particularly in his concern over his declining sexual prowess. There is a tragic vulnerability in Othello that makes him an easy prey to Iago's machinations. Although Leontes is modeled on Othello, *The Winter's Tale* has a strongly romantic thrust. It moves toward the sixteen-year gap and the happy ending of the statue scene (5.3), which celebrates the warmth of married love.

Chapter 9 concerns old warriors and statesmen in the English history plays. Talbot in *1 Henry VI* and Clifford in *2 Henry VI* are two heroic warriors who look forward to the exploits of King Henry V. Two old statesmen, John of Gaunt in *Richard II* and Cardinal Wolsey in *Henry VIII*, develop tragic potentialities. The dying Gaunt prophesies about the decayed state of England under his nephew, Richard II, but his prophetic words are ignored. The fall of Cardinal Wolsey in *Henry VIII* reflects the tragedy of a greedy and ambitious man who misjudges the king's marriage wishes. Nevertheless, Wolsey's reputation is rehabilitated following his death.

Chapter 10 deals with the fatal attraction of Antony and Cleopatra. Both characters are represented as old and experienced. Cleopatra is cunning and histrionic as a lover. Antony is deeply concerned about his dotage and his idleness and the fact that "authority melts from me" (3.13.90). In the play the fall of Antony is powerfully represented by imagery of melting and dissolution. To this end the play uses a unique lexicon of words prefixed by "dis," such as "dislimn" and "discandy."

Chapter 11 focuses on the many strong older women in Shakespeare. Volumnia in *Coriolanus* is a good example of an authoritative patrician who establishes the aristocratic, military values of the play, yet she cannot persuade her son, Marcius, to compromise these values in order to be elected consul. He is thus exiled from Rome. Queen Margaret in the *Henry VI* plays and in *Richard III* serves as the voice of history and moral conscience in reminding us of the crimes of Richard, Duke of Gloucester, who later becomes King Richard III. In her choral role she develops into a tedious scold bent on revenge. Like Queen Margaret, the Duchess of York, who is Richard's mother, curses her own misbegotten son. Gertrude in *Hamlet* is an ambiguous figure, but in the closet scene (3.4) Hamlet seems to absolve her of complicity in his father's murder. The Witches and Hecate in *Macbeth* are other strong, monstrous women who tease Macbeth about his future. They are referred to as the "weird" sisters, or instrumentalities of fate.

Chapter 12 is devoted to older loving women. The best example is the Countess of Rousillon in *All's Well That Ends Well*. Helena, the daughter of the late Gerard de Narbon, is under the guardianship of the countess, who professes a strong maternal affection for her, especially since she is in love with Bertram, the countess's son. Helena fears committing incest, but the countess is fully aware of the distinction between daughter and daughter-in-law. Bertram is a wayward son who shirks his arranged marriage to Helena and sets up oracular conditions for his reappearance. Although the countess is disturbed by her son's erratic conduct, everything turns out well in the end and the marriage is patched up. Hermione is another loving mother and wife in *The Winter's Tale,* but as a polychromed statue in the final scene of the play her speaking part is naturally limited. In this chapter I focus on Paulina, whom Leontes calls an "old turtle," who eventually marries Camillo, Leontes' chief counselor at the beginning of the play. Katherine, the wife of the king in *Henry VIII,* recalls Hermione, especially in their trial scenes. She is a loving, perfect wife, as the king freely admits, but he is determined to marry Anne Bullen. One could also add the abbess Emilia in *The Comedy of Errors,* who is a loving mother to her son Antipholus, whom everyone thinks mad.

Chapter 13 deals with lusty older women, beginning with Dame Quickly of the *Henry IV* plays, *Henry V,* and *The Merry Wives of Windsor.* She speaks in a vigorous, colloquial style, the implication being that she is illiterate and has learned to speak phonetically. The Nurse in *Romeo and Juliet* is also a lower-class character whose speech is rambling, garrulous, and vivid. Tamora in *Titus Andronicus* is obviously not lower class, but she is sexual and dominating. Her role as the allegorical goddess Revenge come from the underworld is misguided because she never believes that the cunning Titus is not mad. To this group one might add the lustful goddess Venus in *Venus and Adonis.* Although her age is never specified, she gives the impression of an importunate, aging woman in hot pursuit of a sexual liaison with the virginal youth Adonis.

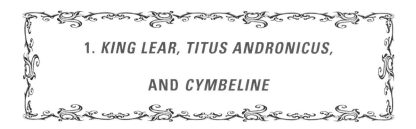

1. *KING LEAR, TITUS ANDRONICUS,* AND *CYMBELINE*

King Lear is the most important play for a study of aging in Shakespeare.[1] *Titus Andronicus* anticipates some of the effects found in *King Lear,* and *Cymbeline* briefly echoes the earlier play. *King Lear* presents conflicting aspects of the old man character, revealing both his foolishness and the wisdom that is gained through suffering. We see Lear at the end of his reign, trying to abdicate yet unwilling to part with "the name, and all th'addition to a king" (1.1.137). This is an impossible contradiction, and the love test he imposes on his daughters is a sign of approaching senility. Can he retain his authority or is he an "idle old man"? The conflict between these opposing impulses involves Lear in a tragedy that is close to the idea of tragedy developed in Aristotle's *Poetics*. All three old men in each of the plays share distinct similarities.

The various issues in *King Lear* are immediately present in the first scene of the play. The old king of Britain is clearly vain and petulant as he prepares to abdicate and divide his kingdom among his three daughters. Before the love test even begins, we know that he has reserved the choicest share for his youngest daughter, Cordelia, whom he consults last. Yet the question on which so much depends is foolish in the extreme: "Which of you shall we say doth love us most?" (1.1.51). Both Goneril and Regan deploy the empty rhetoric one expects of them. Only Cordelia has nothing to say: "What shall Cordelia speak? Love, and be silent" (62). This is an uncomfortable, embarrassing scene because everyone seems to be aware of Lear's folly and the fact that these speeches are merely rhetorical displays.

This point is driven home by the acerbic and loveless remarks of Goneril and Regan at the end of the scene. Although they win all, they know exactly what is going on, and their utter contempt for their old father anticipates what will happen in the play. Their conversation suggests that they are talking about a subject they have often discussed. It is chilling to realize how completely they agree with each other. Goneril first expresses her obvious dissatisfaction with her father, who is clearly losing control and growing senile: "You see how full of changes his age is. The observation we have made of it hath not been little. He always loved our sister most, and with what poor judgment he hath now cast her off appears too grossly" (290–93).

Like other villains in Shakespeare, Goneril possesses keen insight. Cordelia is Lear's perennial favorite, his love child. Their father's great gift of a third of his kingdom elicits no gratitude from Goneril. Instead, she sees it as a sign of his failing judgment. All of this is grossly apparent. Unlike Kent, neither sister has made the least effort to tell her father what she really thinks of him, or to prevent the unfair division of the kingdom and the disinheritance of Cordelia. Goneril remains smug and self-satisfied.

Regan concurs completely: "'Tis the infirmity of his age, yet he hath ever but slenderly known himself" (294–95). This introduces the Aristotelian theme leading to Lear's tragedy. *King Lear* is the play closest to the idea of anagnorisis, or recognition, in Aristotle's *Poetics*. In other words, like other tragic protagonists, Lear "hath ever but slenderly known himself." By an inevitable process Lear moves past blindness and suffering to self-knowledge. Both Goneril and Regan speak of their father in terms that one would now associate with dementia or Alzheimer's disease. They are preoccupied with his old age and his psychological infirmities: he is "rash," suffers from "the unruly way-wardness that infirm and choleric years bring with them" (299–300), and is given to "unconstant starts" (301)—in other words, he is impulsive and has irrational quirks. Goneril and Regan provide a chilling commentary on the scene we have just witnessed. They vow to "hit" together, to devise a joint strategy for dealing with their aged and incompetent father, who is on the verge of senility and second childhood. We already experience a distinct sense of foreboding in terms of what will happen in the rest of the play.

Having begun at the end of the first scene in order to locate Lear's situation in the frightening perspective of Goneril and Regan, I would now like to go back to an earlier point in the scene where Lear announces his decision to abdicate. The statement of his "darker purpose" (35) is full of irresponsible contradictions. According to the map he has in front of him, he will divide his kingdom into three parts in order

> To shake all cares and business from our age,
> Conferring them on younger strengths, while we
> Unburdened crawl toward death. (38–40)

Lear is preoccupied with his age, and he seems to acknowledge that he is no longer capable of ruling his kingdom. The image of crawling toward death is the first of many references suggesting second childhood. The theme of infantilization becomes more obvious in his relations with Goneril and Regan, but it is especially pronounced in Lear's dealings with the Fool. Lear speaks of the division of the kingdom as an act of divestiture "both of rule,/Interest of territory, cares of state" (49–50).

He is eager to be a free man, a private citizen, but he doesn't understand his impulses the way Goneril and Regan do. He angrily disowns his daughter Cordelia because she doesn't say what he wants to hear.

He readily disposes of her ample third to her sisters, and he lays out the terms and conditions of his retirement as if it were a legal contract:

> I do invest you jointly with my power,
> Pre-eminence and all the large effects
> That troop with majesty. (131–33)

Lear excepts his retinue of a hundred knights and makes the stipulation that he shall reside by turns with his two daughters. The next line therefore comes as a shock when he states "only we shall retain / The name, and all th'addition to a king" (136–37). What Lear is proposing is something like Richard II's transformation into a "mockery king of snow" in his deposition scene (4.1.259). How can Lear abdicate his kingship yet retain all the titles and honors of a king? Goneril and Regan haven't the slightest intention of fulfilling this illogical contractual stipulation. The issues of the play are thus clearly outlined in the first scene.

Goneril and Regan know exactly what they are doing. To readers of Shakespeare's history plays their plotting represents a conspiracy against their old father. By the third scene Goneril is actively encouraging her servant Oswald's negligence. This is how she describes her father:

> Idle old man,
> That still would manage those authorities
> That he hath given away. (17–19)

"Idle" is a multivalent term in Elizabethan discourse. It can mean both "without occupation" and "foolish," as if the foolishness is a product of having nothing to do. "Idle" fits in well here since Lear's marginalization is the result of his own choice.

Goneril's speech turns on our understanding of "authorities" and what constitutes authority. One thinks of Antony in *Antony and Cleopatra*, who, when he sees Thidias kiss Cleopatra's hand, realizes that "authority melts from me" (3.13.90). Lear is preoccupied with the loss of authority, which is a natural part of the "addition," or title, of a king. This is echoed in Lear's madness when he meets Gloucester near Dover. The farmer's dog barks at a beggar and the latter runs from the cur, which illustrates "the great image of authority: a dog's obeyed in office" (4.6.154–55). In other words, even a dog commands obedience when he is performing his duty (or "office"), just as the king will be obeyed merely because he is a monarch.

These are among the first exchanges that the disguised Kent speaks to Lear when he is seeking to become his servant:

> LEAR: Dost thou know me, fellow?
> KENT: No, sir, but you have that in your countenance which I
> would fain call master.
> LEAR: What's that?
> KENT: Authority. (1.4.26–30)

Kent validates Lear's desire to be every inch a king. This points to a central question of the play: Has the abdicated Lear become an idle old man or does he still manifest his kingly authority? R. A. Foakes's insistence that Lear maintains all the accoutrements of royalty and should not be presented as a Beckettian beggar provides an important answer to this question.[2]

Goneril is absolutely clear about her father's reversion to second childhood: "Old fools are babes again and must be used / With checks as flatteries, when they are seen abused" (1.3.30–31). As the controlling words "checks" and "flatteries" imply, one must deal with senile old men exactly as one would with babies. In the next scene the bitter Fool takes up Goneril's discourse on senility, confronting Lear with his utter foolishness, since he has done it all voluntarily: "Thou hadst little wit in thy bald crown when thou gav'st thy golden one away" (1.4.155–56). Lear threatens the Fool with the whip, but the latter invokes the license of his office and is impervious to the king's threats. He speaks bluntly and without mitigation, claiming "thou mad'st thy daughters thy mothers . . . when thou gav'st them the rod and putt'st down thine own breeches" (163–65). Lacking his former authority, Lear is once again a babe who needs to be disciplined with beatings (the rod)—just as now he threatens the Fool.

The Fool drives home his point when Goneril enters:

> Thou wast a pretty fellow when thou hadst no need to care for her frowning. Now thou art an O without a figure; I am better than thou art now. I am a fool, thou art nothing. (182–85)

"Nothing" is a crucial term in Act 1, starting with Cordelia's surprising "Nothing, my lord" (87). By surrendering his kingship, Lear has lost all power. He has become anonymous, a nonentity, like Richard II, who confesses: "I have no name, no title, / No, not that name was given me at the font" (4.1.254–55). The pathos arises from Lear's self-deprivation of everything that gives him value as a king and as a man. His struggle to recover his status and his integrity is what the play is all about—and, of course, he never does. His threat to "resume the shape which thou dost think / I have cast off for ever" (1.4.301–2) is mere bravado.

Another significant term in this scene is "dotage," which Goneril uses to describe her old father to Albany: "let his disposition have that scope / As dotage gives it" (284–85). Like the word "idle," "dotage" has a dual meaning. It generally refers to old lovers who love excessively, or "dote" on their lady loves. Old lovers are generally uxorious and love their wives beyond all measure. Earlier in the scene Kent tells Lear that he is "not so young, sir, to love a woman for singing, nor so old to dote on her for anything" (37–38). And early in *Antony and Cleopatra* Antony declares: "These strong Egyptian fetters I must break / Or lose myself in dotage" (1.2.117–18). Notice that dotage is represented in terms of chains.

"Dotage" can also refer to the loss of one's cognitive powers, as in second childhood. Goneril is literally disempowering her father. A few lines down the issue becomes Lear's personal retinue of one hundred knights. Goneril projects a baseless political fear: "He may enguard his dotage with their powers / And hold our lives in mercy" (319–20). At this point Lear has become impotent; he can only inveigh against his daughters in highflown, rhetorical terms:

> Ingratitude, thou marble-hearted fiend
> More hideous when thou show'st thee in a child
> Than the sea-monster. (251–53)

Or again:

> How sharper than a serpent's tooth it is
> To have a thankless child. (280–81)

These exclamations provide one way of understanding Lear's tragedy. Aside from insult and humiliation, Goneril and Regan violate nature and natural law (as does Edmund vis-à-vis his father Gloucester). They sever the deep bond that exists between parent and child. The ruthlessness and heartlessness of Goneril and Regan are what disturb us and elicit enormous sympathy and compassion for the foolish and suffering Lear, who has given everything away of his own free but misguided will.

Shakespeare pushes the abasement and humiliation of Lear to an extreme degree by placing him out on the heath in the wind and the rain, amid thunder and lightning. Clothing imagery expresses the hypocrisy of the world: "Robes and furred gowns hide all" (4.6.161), whereas the truth is naked, proverbial, and elemental. The ragged Edgar as Poor Tom is the symbol of natural man: "Thou ow'st the worm no silk, the beast no hide, the sheep no wool, the cat no perfume. Ha? Here's three on's are sophisticated; thou art the thing itself. Unaccommodated man is no more but such a poor, bare, forked animal as thou art" (3.4.101–6).

It is at this point that Lear tears off his clothes: "Off, off, you lendings: come, unbutton here" (106–7). This is a crucial moment in the representation of Lear as a decrepit old man, shivering with cold. It is a great moment for actors. The disrobed old man onstage evokes a good measure of Aristotelian catharsis, the pity and fear that lie at the heart of tragedy.

The return of Lear to sanity is marked by a change in costume. They "put fresh garments on him" (4.7.22). He is bewildered because he thinks he has been taken out of his grave and snatched from the torments of hell:

> I am bound
> Upon a wheel of fire that mine own tears
> Do scald like molten lead. (46–48)

As he talks with his much-wronged daughter Cordelia, he shows a new humility:

> I am a very foolish, fond old man,
> Fourscore and upward, not an hour more or less;
> And to deal plainly,
> I fear I am not in my perfect mind. (60–63)

"Fond" means foolish, idle, doting. We feel that Lear is at the extreme edge of life. He humbly craves his daughter's pardon: "You must bear with me. Pray you now, forget and forgive; I am old and foolish" (83–84). In his last speech he seems to be suffocating when he asks an attendant: "Pray you undo this button. Thank you, sir" (5.3.308). This is followed in the quarto version of the play by four O-groans, which are similar to the five O-groans at the end of *Hamlet* in the folio version.[3] These function as a kind of death cry in both plays.

The theme of Lear as an old man is echoed in the subplot by the figure of Gloucester. The Lear and Gloucester parallel actions are played off against each other and strengthen the role of aging in the play. In act 1, scene 2, Edmund's fictitious letter from his brother Edgar raises issues that resemble the revolt of Goneril and Regan against their father in the first scene of the play. It is clear that Edmund has the same pernicious ideas as Lear's two eldest daughters. Gloucester is horrified as he reads Edgar's spurious letter: "I begin to find an idle and fond bondage in the oppression of aged tyranny, who sways not as it hath power, but as it suffered" (49–51). Note the words "idle" and "fond," which Edmund seems to borrow from the Lear action. Edgar hints that he is ready to murder his father and appropriate his revenues. Gloucester interprets the letter in relation to the "late eclipses in the sun and moon" (103). His sense of a general global malaise recalls Hamlet's first soliloquy: "How weary, stale, flat, and unprofitable / Seem to me all the uses of the world!" (1.2.133–34). Gloucester provides the play with an appropriately pessimistic context: "This villain of mine comes under the prediction—there's son against father. The King falls from bias of nature—there's father against child. We have seen the best of our time" (1.2.109–12).

Although Gloucester's age is never specified—Shakespeare is generally reluctant to provide specific ages—he is always referred to as white-haired. Like Lear he is old and foolish, boastful of his sexual prowess in engendering the bastard Edmund, and quick to believe Edmund's plot against his brother. In one of the cruelest scenes in all of Shakespeare, the blinding of Gloucester is presented onstage, with each eye separately extinguished. The suffering of Gloucester is analogous to the suffering of Lear during the storm on the heath, and both protagonists elicit our pity.

We are made acutely conscious of Gloucester's aged body as Regan plucks white hairs from his beard and urges her husband, Cornwall, to bind him "hard, hard. O, filthy traitor" (3.7.32). Cornwall directs a servant to "bind fast his corky arms" (29). This is the only occurrence of "corky" in all of Shakespeare. It refers to Gloucester's limp, spindly, withered arms. The physical cruelty of this scene is unendurable, and Shakespeare does nothing to mitigate its effects. The good-hearted Gloucester inveighs against the savagery of Regan and Goneril to their father; he has sent Lear to Dover

Because I would not see thy cruel nails
Pluck out his poor old eyes; nor thy fierce sister
In his anointed flesh stick boorish fangs. (55–57)

Gloucester's speech offers a hint to Cornwall to set his foot on Gloucester's eyes and stamp them out, but he does so only for one eye, the other being plucked out: "Out, vile jelly / Where is thy luster now?" (82–83). The blinded and despairing Gloucester is led out onto the heath by a nameless Old Man of "fourscore years" (4.1.15).

The most affecting scene in the play occurs when the blind Gloucester meets the mad Lear in the fields near Dover. Lear immediately recognizes him: "Ha! Goneril with a white beard?" (4.6.96). Later Lear takes him for "blind Cupid" (134) and swears he himself will not fall in love. Edgar typically points up the emotional and moral tone of this meeting:

> I would not take this from report; it is,
> And my heart breaks at it. (137–38)

When Lear exits, Gloucester confirms that he is cured of his despair:

> You ever gentle gods, take my breath from me;
> Let not my worser spirit tempt me again
> To die before you please. (213–15)

Presumably Gloucester no longer believes "as flies to wanton boys are we to the gods, / They kill us for their sport" (4.1.38–39).

Although he is only forty-eight as he presents himself in disguise to be Lear's servant, Kent is represented as a third old man in the play. He is definitely not an old man by contemporary standards, but in Shakespeare's time fifty generally marked the beginning of old age for men. When Lear asks Kent how old he is, Kent in disguise shows himself as a forthright, blunt man; his answer sounds proverbial: "Not so young, sir, to love a woman for singing nor so old to dote on her for anything. I have years on my back forty-eight" (1.4.37–39). This fits in well with the "old man as dotard" theme. In the first scene Kent violently objects to Lear's decision to disinherit Cordelia, as a result of which he is banished. Even before Goneril and Regan discuss their father's approaching senility, Kent emphasizes how much Lear's judgment has been compromised by old age:

> What wouldst thou do, old man?
> Think'st thou that duty shall have dread to speak,
> When power to flattery bows? (1.1.147–49)

In disguise as Lear's servant, Kent plays a role like the Fool's, namely, to remind Lear of his folly. Old men are gullible; Lear's need to be loved makes him particularly susceptible to flattery.

When Kent outfaces Oswald and beats him in act 2, scene 2, and then is placed in the stocks by Cornwall, there is strong emphasis on old age. Oswald refers to him as "this ancient ruffian, sir, whose life I have spared at suit of his grey beard" (60–61), and Cornwall speaks of him as an "old fellow" (83) and "you stubborn, ancient knave, you reverend braggart" (124). Despite the fact that Kent is a bit more than half Lear's age, it is significant that in the context of the play he is made to seem much older. This is undoubtedly done to strengthen our perception of Lear and Gloucester as even older than Kent and much more frail.

At the end of the last scene of the play, it seems as if Kent, like Gloucester and Lear, will die: "I have a journey, sir, shortly to go; / My master calls me, I must not say no" (5.3.320–21). The play ends with Edgar's couplets (in folio) separating the young from the old: "The oldest hath borne most; we that are young / Shall never see so much, nor live so long" (324–25). Edgar makes it seem as if the conflict between youth and age is the tragic theme of the play. The oldest, like Lear and Gloucester, have "borne most," meaning that they have suffered and experienced the most. The young shall never be able to live life as fully as Lear and Gloucester or attain the tragic wisdom that comes through suffering. When Edgar says that the young will not "live so long," he seems to imply not that they will not live so many years—Lear is fourscore and upward—but that they will not live such profound and meaningful lives.

Titus Andronicus anticipates *King Lear* in several respects.[4] Both plays are intensely passionate, and Titus's madness resolves issues that will be more fully developed in the later play. There are also some similarities between Titus's daughter Lavinia and Cordelia in *King Lear*. Although the Clown in *Titus Andronicus* has a very minor role compared to that of the Fool in *King Lear*, both are nevertheless integral to the action of the plays. In both plays the crucial downfall of the protagonists is completed in the first scene of the first act. Titus's refusal of the crown is presented as a grave error having dire consequences, as is the folly of Lear's love test and his rejection of Cordelia, the daughter whom he clearly loves the most. Both Titus and Lear are presented as old men whose judgment is impaired. Lear is fourscore and upward. Titus has been Rome's soldier for forty years. He has buried twenty-one of his valiant sons, all of whom fought in his country's wars, with only four still living. He must be at least sixty, although he is consistently represented in the play as much older.

Titus refuses the crown that is offered to him by his brother, Marcus, because he is sure that he is too old for kingship: "A better head her [Rome's] glorious body fits / Than his that shakes for age and feebleness" (1.1.187–88). These are curious lines since Titus has just returned to Rome in a glorious triumphal procession. The character we see before us onstage is hardly palsied with age and feebleness but rather intensely martial and heroic. Similarly, in the first scene of the play Lear is not palsied or feeble. He is hardly ready

> To shake all cares and business from our age,
> Conferring them on younger strengths, while we
> Unburdened crawl toward death. (1.1.38–40)

It seems self-indulgent and inappropriate for Titus to ask for "a staff of honor for mine age, / But not a scepter to control the world" (1.1.198–99). Titus's comparison of himself to King Priam in the *Iliad* (he is also an important figure in "Aeneas's tale to Dido" in *Hamlet,* 2.2) should alert us to his later claims to aged feebleness. Priam, like Anchises, the father of Aeneas, was a type of the frail, defenseless, impotent old man.

Titus's suffering begins immediately in the first scene of the play as the action proceeds swiftly against him. He foolishly and impulsively kills his own son, Mutius, and soon becomes acutely aware of his diminished status:

> I am not bid to wait upon this bride [Tamora].
> Titus, when wert thou wont to walk alone,
> Dishonored thus and challenged of wrongs? (1.1.339–41)

This is spoken in a soliloquy. By the end of the scene Titus is weary of life. He reluctantly agrees to the burial of his son Mutius in the family vault as if nothing matters anymore: "Well, bury him, and bury me the next" (387). Tamora deceptively indulges him as "this good old man" (458).

When Titus pleads with the judges and senators (3.1) to spare his two sons, who are about to be executed, he is already frantic, overwrought, and close to madness. His emotional state resembles that of Lear. Both old men cannot cope with the new reality confronting them. Titus puts great emphasis on his feeble old age. He pleads with the tribunes "for pity of mine age" (2) and speaks of "these bitter tears, which now you see / Filling the agèd wrinkles of my cheeks" (6–7). In staged representations the audience presumably needs to see a very different Titus from that of the returning warrior in the triumphal procession of the first scene. This should also hold true for the way in which Lear is represented. He must be made to seem much wearier and frailer than he was at the beginning of the play.

Titus lies down on the stage and pretends to write "My heart's deep languor" (13) with the warm tears that fall from his eyes, "these two ancient ruins" (17). This image seems to be recalled in *Richard II* when the protagonist despairingly exclaims:

> Let's talk of graves, of worms, and epitaphs,
> Make dust our paper, and with rainy eyes
> Write sorrow on the bosom of the earth. (3.2.145–47)

Titus seems to be close to death at this point, which runs parallel to his sense of losing his reason. He describes his hands as "with red herbs" (177) and personifies himself as the sea (225). The scene reaches its climax with his frantic outburst "Ha, ha, ha!" (264). Like Lear, Titus's rage is monumental and uncontrollable. In an attempt at reasonableness, he explains to his brother that he is laughing because "I have not another tear to shed" (266).

The fly scene (3.2) shows us a Titus who is clearly distracted. Is he really mad? This intriguing question recurs in several of Shakespeare's plays. Ophelia in *Hamlet* definitely runs lunatic and never recovers her wits. In *The Two Noble Kinsmen* the Jailer's Daughter, who is modeled on Ophelia, runs mad for love but eventually recovers. Lear also appears to recover his wits (5.3), but he seems to be returning from a very distant, otherwordly place. At this point he is a broken man about to die. There is the greatest degree of ambiguity in the character of Hamlet. Like Titus, he is represented as frantic, distracted, and overwrought emotionally, but he is hardly lunatic like Ophelia. I think this distinction is important because madness, or the "antic disposition" (1.5.172) that Hamlet deliberately assumes, allows for a tremendous widening and deepening of his role emotionally, philosophically, and lyrically. The fly scene in *Titus Andronicus* is so unusual for early Shakespeare that its authorship has been questioned, yet the point of the scene is precisely to expand and endow the character of Titus with greater complexity.

Scene 2 of act 3 follows directly from the strong emotions aroused in the previous scene. Like Lear, Titus is approaching the breaking point. He is fully aware of "how frantically I square my talk" (31). The black fly is, of course, a symbol of Aaron, Tamora's beloved moor, in all his homicidal viciousness. Titus's lines manage to combine an absurd personification of the fly with a lyric frenzy that strikes at the heart of his monumental grief:

> "But!" How if that fly had a father and mother?
> How would he hang his slender gilded wings,
> And buzz lamenting doings in the air! (60–62)

Like Lear, Titus is an old man who possesses an entirely different mind-set from that of the rational characters in the play. His brother, Marcus, who functions as a kind of raisonneur in the play, can only commiserate with Titus: "Alas, poor man! Grief has so wrought on him, / He takes false shadows for true substances" (79–80). Titus's madness, however, offers him a brutal insight into the nature of things that was entirely lacking earlier.

By act 4, scene 4, Tamora is boasting of her ability to manipulate the aged and mad Titus. This scene prepares us for her fateful and utterly mistaken role as Revenge in act 5, scene 2, where she is attended by her sons, personifying Rape and Murder. In the earlier scene Tamora—in her motherly role as wife and counselor to her much younger husband, Saturninus—is confident that she knows exactly how to handle Titus. She will enchant him "With words more sweet, and yet more dangerous, / Than baits to fish or honey-stalks [clover] to sheep"(91–92). She will "fill his agèd ears / With golden promises" (97–98). Of course, Tamora's confidence is overweening and eventually leads to the deaths of her two sons, with whose dismembered bodies Titus fills a pie that is greedily devoured by their clueless mother.

This scene reaches its climax in act 5, scene 2. Tamora, as Revenge, is shrewd enough to capitalize on Titus's preoccupation with justice and his urgent attempt to force Justice personified to emerge from the underworld. But Titus, although overwrought, is clearly not mad. Tamora may be claiming "to ease the gnawing vulture" (31) of his mind, but Titus asserts unequivocally:

I am not mad, I know thee well enough.
Witness this wretched stump, witness these crimson lines,
Witness these trenches made by grief and care,
Witness the tiring day and heavy night,
Witness all sorrow, that I know thee well
For our proud empress, mighty Tamora. (5.2.21–26)

Irrespective of what Titus says, Tamora remains convinced of his "lunacy" (70). In fact, she is so sure of herself that she leaves her sons with him. In a significant aside Titus triumphantly asserts his sanity and hints at his hideous revenge:

I knew them all, though they supposed me mad;
And will o'erreach them in their own devices,
A pair of cursed hellhounds and their dame. (142–44)

Throughout the scene Tamora and her sons treat Titus as a mad and impotent old man. They patronize him as if he were a child.

After Titus has been killed by Saturninus in the next scene (5.3), an old Roman lord acts as a spokesman for the dead hero. His "frosty signs" [white hair] and "chaps of age" [wrinkled skin] are "grave witnesses of true experience" (77–78). He invokes King Priam and the fall of Troy as an analogue to the events in Rome. Titus is grandsire to Lucius's son, who will recount the "pretty tales" his grandfather told him and "talk of them when he was dead and gone" (165–66). In her film adaptation of *Titus Andronicus,* director Julie Taymor utilizes Lucius's son's point of view as a framing device to present the action of the play.

Cymbeline resembles King Lear even more closely than Titus. He is an old, white-haired king of pre-Roman Britain, and his daughter, Imogen, with whom he is angry, is like Lear's daughter Cordelia. He is vexed by his daughter's reference to his declining years:

O disloyal thing
That shouldst repair my youth, thou heap'st
A year's age on me. (1.1.132–34)

Presumably "a year's age" is an age of years, meaning that Imogen is making her father seem very old. Cymbeline doesn't reappear until act 2, scene 3, and his role in the play is truncated and underdeveloped. At the end of the play, however, he is joyously reunited with his daughter, just as Lear is reunited with Cordelia. Shakespeare must have had *King Lear* in mind when he wrote *Cymbeline*, although the king doesn't have a very vital role in this play.

More developed than Cymbeline as an old father is Belarius, a banished lord. His sons, Guiderius and Arviragus, are actually the kidnapped children of Cymbeline, and they are restored to their rightful father at the end of the play. These events occurred twenty years ago. Guiderius speaks of his father's "stiff age" (3.3.32). Before he banished him, Cymbeline loved Belarius:

> Then was I as a tree
> Whose boughs did bend with fruit. But in one night
> A storm or robbery, call it what you will,
> Shook down my mellow hangings, nay, my leaves,
> And left me bare to weather. (60–64)

The image of old age as a leafless tree in winter is familiar from the "Bare ruined choirs" of Sonnet 73. At the end of the play Belarius is the "ancient soldier" (5.3.15) Posthumus speaks of, the white-bearded old man he rescues. Belarius is much more fully developed as a character then Cymbeline, and his old age tends to confirm that of the king.

One should also mention the ghostly figure of Posthumus's father, Sicilius Leonatus, whom Shakespeare describes as *an old man attired like a warrior; leading in his hand an ancient Matron, his wife and mother to Posthumus"* (5.4.29). These figures, conjured by Posthumus in his sleep, lead to Jupiter's vision and final judgment. They are an important aspect of the final representation of old age in the play. *Cymbeline* places strong emphasis on a generational divide between young and old, which is ultimately removed by the end of the play.

King Lear, Titus Andronicus, and, to a lesser extent, Cymbeline are all old men whose irrationality determines the outcome of their respective plays. However, Lear is a much more complex character than either Titus or Cymbeline. An old man who possesses all the infirmities of old age (e.g., petulance, irascibility, and misogyny), his need for flattery and love is insatiable. We nevertheless feel his tragedy intensely because his suffering is beyond all measure; it is excessive in relation to the faults usually associated with old age. Titus, the great Roman military hero, similarly experiences suffering that goes beyond any sense of moral equivalence. His consent to the human sacrifice of Tamora's son Alarbus at the beginning of the play precipitates a downward spiral that, like a whirlpool, sucks Titus and his daughter into its vicious swirls. These events endow Lear and Titus with an acute sense of tragedy associated with old age.

2. THE AGING PROCESS,

WITH SPECIAL REFERENCE TO *MACBETH*

The topic of growing old in Shakespeare is closely connected with the representation of time in the plays. It is obvious that there is a sharp contrast between the time projected by the narrative and the time imagined to have elapsed during a specific scene. This has sometimes been called "double time,"[1] or long and short time, to account for its duality. It is similar to the use of montage in cinema. In other words, small sections of the narrative are pieced together into concentrated scenes or "takes." Also, there are many verbal references to time that can't be neatly worked out mathematically, such as Othello's remark, after he has murdered Desdemona, "That she with Cassio hath the act of shame / A thousand times committed" (5.2.208–9).

This is quite different from the extensive development of narrative in fiction, which usually proceeds chronologically to tell its story. In Shakespeare characters seem to age in relation to the logic of the dramatic action rather than the logical progression of the narrative. That may explain why Shakespeare generally avoids specifying the amount of time that has elapsed. Except in plays where unity of time is important, like *The Comedy of Errors* and *The Tempest*, Shakespeare prefers to be vague about how much time has elapsed. In *Romeo and Juliet*, however, the hours and the days are accounted for with surprising exactness in order to increase our sense of suspense.

Characters grow older—or, more accurately, mature—as they face important decisions. This is clearly true of Juliet in *Romeo and Juliet*. As she is progressively abandoned by her father, her mother, and even her nurse, she readies herself psychologically to take Friar Lawrence's potion, perhaps even to confront death, as she surmises. Her new resolve makes her seem much older and more mature than the not quite fourteen-year-old girl earlier in the play. In her long soliloquy (4.3.14–58) she speaks with a firmness of purpose and a lucidity that resemble the meditative soliloquies in *Hamlet*. She realizes that "my dismal scene I needs must act alone" (19) and places a dagger by her side in case the potion doesn't work. She prepares herself for a suicide similar to Cleopatra's, "after the high Roman fashion" (*Antony and Cleopatra*, 4.15.86). She eventually overcomes her profound fear and exclaims ecstatically: "Romeo, Romeo, Romeo, I drink to thee" (4.3.58). Youth and age are firmly opposed in this early tragedy. The parents of Romeo and Juliet are made to seem excessively old, with their hopes for the future shattered by their "ancient grudge" (3), as the Prologue states.

Likewise in *Hamlet* there are a few scattered references to the specific age of the protagonist. At the beginning of the play Hamlet, a university student at Wittenberg, is suddenly called home as a result of his father's untimely death. In the gravedigger's scene toward the end of the play (5.1) we learn that the clown-gravedigger has been a sexton for thirty years. He has just dug up the skull of Yorick, the king's jester, which "hath lien you i' th' earth three and twenty years" (174–75). Hamlet takes the skull in his hands and reminisces about "poor Yorick," who "hath borne me on his back a thousand times" (187–88). So how old does that make Hamlet at that precise moment? If one bothered to do the math (which audiences never have time to do), Hamlet must now be about thirty years old. Does that mean that at least ten years have passed since the opening of the play, when Hamlet was still a student at Wittenberg? I feel that these are idle and unprofitable speculations, but what is important is that Hamlet now seems much older than he did when the play began. He has a new seriousness and sense of purpose. Like Juliet, he seems to have grown older and more mature. In the next scene with Horatio (5.2) Hamlet believes "there's a divinity that shapes our ends, / Rough-hew them how we will" (10–11). Later Hamlet defies augury: "There is a special providence in the fall of a sparrow. If it be now, 'tis not to come; if it be not to come, it will be now; if it be not now, yet it will come. The readiness is all" (220–24). This does not at all sound like the meditative speech of a university student newly returned from Wittenberg. In fact, it sounds like the theologically tinged speech of an aging student recently returned from Martin Luther's university. The proverbial phrase "the readiness is all" anticipates Edgar's homiletic "Ripeness is all" in *King Lear* (5.2.11). According to an inevitable natural law and without any human intervention, fruit falls from the tree when it is ripe.

There are numerous hints throughout Shakespeare that age is determined psychologically and in relation to the dramatic context. In *Richard II*, for example, the frivolous, capricious, self-willed king of the earlier part of the play is made to disappear in the later scenes, when Richard is imprisoned and awaits his inevitable execution. Already in act 5, scene 1, the deposed Richard is lamenting his fate and anticipating his death. As he tells his queen:

> In winter's tedious nights sit by the fire
> With good old folks, and let them tell thee tales
> Of woeful ages long ago betid;
> And ere thou bid good night, to quite [requite] their griefs
> Tell thou the lamentable tale of me,
> And send the hearers weeping to their beds. (40–45)

Winter, a winter's tale, night, and "ages long ago betid" are all part of the conventional imagery of old age confronting death.

In his dungeon cell Richard continues these direful meditations. Now that he is "unkinged by Bolingbroke" (5.5.37), he has lost his identity. His long speech on the nature of time conveys a strong psychological feeling of despairing old age: "I wasted time, and now doth Time waste me: / For now hath Time made me his numb'ring clock" (49–50).

I have been arguing that the feeling of growing old in Shakespeare is strongly connected with the sense of adversity and reversal of fortune. Characters seem to mature suddenly when they are faced with important decisions. It is quite clear that Shakespeare as a dramatist is not concerned with chronological time. He tends to avoid specific mention of the ages of his characters and the amount of time that has elapsed in the dramatic action. The sense of aging in Shakespeare is marked by jumps and discontinuities. The before-and-after paradigm occurs often in the plays because it offers a way of highlighting psychological contrast. Duality is central to Shakespearean structure. This is certainly true of *Richard II* and *Hamlet*, which depend on an earlier/later dichotomy. *The Winter's Tale,* with Time acting as chorus, literally projects a long interval of sixteen years between the earlier and later parts. This is also true of *Pericles,* with Gower acting as chorus.

Timon of Athens presents a sharp delineation between Timon during prosperity and adversity. Does he seem to grow old in the later part of the play? An illusion of aging is conveyed by the kind of imagery he uses for his bitter misanthropy. For example, in his first long soliloquy outside the walls of Athens Timon exploits the negative imagery of disease and decrepitude:

> Son of sixteen,
> Pluck the lined crutch from thy old limping sire,
> With it beat out his brains. (4.1.13–15)

The senators, who have already been presented as old and doddering, are the objects of Timon's bitter curse:

> Thou cold sciatica,
> Cripple our senators, that their limbs may halt
> As lamely as their manners. (23–25)

In imagistic terms, Timon as a character absorbs the baleful representations of his curses. In other words, his imagery of old age and disease is self-reflexive for the speaker. Timon creates the illusion that he is an old man preoccupied with the physical infirmities of old age. He appears decrepit in his misanthropy because he imitates the style and subject matter of a decrepit old man. Concerning the appeal of the senators, who plead with him to spare Athens from an attack by Alcibiades, Timon cares not a jot "if he sack fair Athens / And take our goodly aged men by th' beards" (5.1.172–73).

Macbeth offers the best example in Shakespeare of a character who seems to age considerably in the course of the action. Shakespeare is careful not to provide any specific time indications. At the beginning of the play Macbeth is represented as a young, heroic warrior. The "bleeding Captain" reports that the "brave Macbeth" valiantly combatted the "merciless" rebel Macdonwald "till he unseamed him from the nave [navel] to th' chops [jaws], / And fixed his head upon our battlements" (1.2.22–23). At this point Macbeth is still an energetic and optimistic military hero. He doesn't begin to be troubled psychologically until he hears the prophecies by the Witches in the following scene on the "blasted heath" (1.3.77). Macbeth is tempted by the Witches' report and seems to change quickly from the heroic figure he was at the beginning of the play. The possibility of killing King Duncan and crowning himself king—in which he is powerfully encouraged by his wife— seems to age him in an indeterminate way. Of course, no specific amount of time is ever indicated, but the process continues inexorably until it reaches its conclusion in Macbeth's despairing speech at the end of the play: "My way of life / Is fall'n into the sear, the yellow leaf" (5.3.22–23).

How does this process unfold? A series of progressive steps inevitably lead to Macbeth's powerful declaration of weariness: "I have lived long enough" (5.3.22). The bloody murder of Duncan "unsexes" (1.5.42) Lady Macbeth, but even more significantly it initiates the unmanning of Macbeth. From this point on his overwhelming anxiety ages him. The process of murder stretches out "to th' crack of doom" (4.1.117). Banquo and his son, Fleance, must be killed next because, as Macbeth says, "To be thus is nothing but [unless] to be safely thus" (3.1.48). The murder of Macduff is conceived as part of an inevitable but deeply unsatisfying cycle:

> I am in blood
> Stepped in so far that, should I wade no more,
> Returning were as tedious as go o'er. (3.4.137–39)

The appearance of the term "tedious" is extraordinary in this context of a river of blood. Murder for Macbeth is beginning to lose the acutely moral significance of his early soliloquy, where he wonders: "Is this a dagger which I see before me?" (2.1.33). *Tedium vitae* is a sure sign of his despair.

Another highly significant step in Macbeth's spiritual desiccation is his speech to his wife at the end of act 3, scene 2:

> Light thickens, and the crow
> Makes wing to th' rooky wood.
> Good things of day begin to droop and drowse,
> Whiles night's black agents to their preys do rouse. (50–53)

The imagery of night coming on and the flight of the threatening crow are part of a negative image cluster, including winter and imminent old age, portending death. Night is a time for murders, of Banquo and the attempted murder of his son, Fleance. The literal thickening of light at twilight is the prelude to dark deeds, as is the sight of crows hastening to their "rooky," or crow-filled, wood. "Black night" in Sonnet 73 is explicitly equated with "Death's second self, that seals up all in rest."

Macbeth is darkly preparing his wife, his "dearest chuck" (45), for the slaughter of Macduff, his wife, and his children. "Chuck," or chick, is a familiar term of endearment, referring to a domestic bird very different in connotation from the crow. He seems wary of telling his wife directly what he is planning. She clearly doesn't grasp the import of what her husband is saying, as is evident in his final couplet: "Thou marvel'st at my words: but hold thee still; / Things bad begun make strong themselves by ill" (54–55). It is interesting that Macbeth seems to think of his wife as being in a different spiritual state from his own impending despair. He doesn't appear to be aware of her instability and her approaching madness.

By act 5, scene 3, Macbeth is "sick at heart" (19) and reflecting actively on images of his own doom:

> My way of life
> Is fall'n into the sear, the yellow leaf,
> And that which should accompany old age,
> As honor, love, obedience, troops of friends,
> I must not look to have. (22–26)

These are all images of late autumn looking toward winter, when leaves turn yellow and fall. Imagistically winter and old age are linked. What is significant here is Macbeth's sense that he has grown old and that he is approaching death. "Sear" is a word meaning withered and dry, just as the aging body—according to the then prevalent theory of the humors—was thought to have lost its essential moisture. There is a natural association between old men and trees whose leaves are drying up and being blown away.

Sonnet 73 has an analogous type of imagery:

> That time of year thou mayst in me behold
> When yellow leaves, or none, or few, do hang
> Upon those boughs which shake against the cold,
> Bare ruined choirs where late the sweet birds sang.

Of course, the crows who "make wing to th' rooky wood" (3.2.5) do not at all resemble the sweet-voiced songbirds who have disappeared in Sonnet 73. This poem represents a somber consideration of the ravages of time, a familiar theme in Shakespeare's sonnets. Other images of impending mutability in this sonnet are twilight, when the sun is fading in the west, and the ashes that result from the extinguished fires of youth. These are all familiar representations of old age in lyric poetry. Black night is about to appear, which images "Death's second self, that seals up all in rest." Macbeth's awareness of old age and its disappointed promises prepares us for his doom. He is acutely conscious of his own deprivation of the warmth and love that an old man should expect to receive. His vivid images of "mouth-honor" seems to be echoed in Timon's bitter reference to his "mouth-friends" (*Timon of Athens*, 3.6.90).

The culmination of Macbeth's negative imagery occurs in act 5, scene 5, when he hears the news of his wife's death. There is a surprising tone of weariness and indifference in his immediate response: "She should have died hereafter; / There would have been a time for such a word" (17–18). "Should" is ambiguous; it can either be taken to mean that she would inevitably have died in the future or that she ought to have died at some more auspicious time.

The coldness of Macbeth's sentiments is enforced by the despairing speech that follows:

Tomorrow, and tomorrow, and tomorrow
Creeps in this petty pace from day to day,
To the last syllable of recorded time. (19–21)

Time is, as it were, personified as speaking his "last syllable" at the end of the world. Like Time the chorus in act 4 of *The Winter's Tale*, Macbeth is represented as an old man speaking out of the depths of his spiritual aridity. What follows is essentially Macbeth's wish for an end to his meaningless life:

Out, out, brief candle!
Life's but a walking shadow, a poor player
That struts and frets his hour upon the stage
And then is heard no more. It is a tale
Told by an idiot, full of sound and fury
Signifying nothing. (23–28)

It is interesting that Macbeth uses a self-reflexive theatrical image to signify an empty and hollow tale. "Shadow" is a word specifically associated with the theater. As Duke Theseus remarks of the actors in the

"Pyramus and Thisby" play within *A Midsummer Night's Dream*: "The best in this kind are but shadows; and the worst are no worse, if imagination amend them" (5.1.212–13). Actors are insubstantial shadows who, through the doctrine of mimesis, imitate or mimic real people. "Shadow" is also a term for a portrait painting, as Bassanio says in *The Merchant of Venice* when he opens the leaden casket with Portia's picture in it:

> The substance of my praise doth wrong this shadow
> In underprizing it, so far this shadow
> Doth limp behind the substance. (3.2.127–29)

Again, according to the doctrine of mimesis, a painted portrait is only an inadequate representation of a living person. "Shadow" is also associated with the thickening of light at twilight and the approach of night and death.

Like her husband, Lady Macbeth also seems to have grown much older by the end of the play. There are no specific indications of her age, but at her first appearance she is already "unsexing" herself (1.5.42). Presumably her "women's breasts" (48) will no longer function to nurse a baby. This is stated before Macbeth even enters the scene. She is firmly resolved that she and her spouse will kill Duncan. In order to persuade her husband to commit the murder, several scenes later she employs the extremely brutal image of a nursing mother killing her babe. Just as she exhorts Macbeth to be a man, she herself displays a masculine ferocity that is the essence of her psychological effort to unsex herself:

> I have given suck, and know
> How tender 'tis to love the babe that milks me:
> I would, while it was smiling in my face,
> Have plucked my nipple from his boneless gums,
> And dashed the brains out, had I so sworn as you
> Have done to this. (1.7.54–59)

It is clear from this that Lady Macbeth is a woman of child-bearing years.

The sleepwalking scene (5.1) reveals a Lady Macbeth we have not known earlier in the play. She is obviously as mad as Ophelia in *Hamlet*. She enters with a taper, indicating that it is night. A doctor of physic and a Waiting-gentlewoman are in attendance. Revealing her extreme sense of guilt, she is preoccupied not only with a bloodstain ("Out damned spot! Out, I say" [38]), but with its smell: "Here's the smell of the blood still. All the perfumes of Arabia will not / Sweeten this little hand. Oh, oh, oh!" (53–55). This emphatically contradicts her shallow optimism right after the murder of Duncan: "A little water clears us of this deed" (2.2.66). Yet Macbeth already knows what his wife will only discover in her madness:

> Will all great Neptune's ocean wash this blood
> Clean from my hand? No; this my hand will rather
> The multitudinous seas incarnadine,
> Making the green one red. (59–62)

Lady Macbeth has changed radically from the woman glimpsed at the beginning of the play. Although we have no way of knowing how many years are assumed to have elapsed in the course of the play, in the sleepwalking scene she speaks like an old and harried woman who is weary of life.

There are two other old men in *Macbeth*: King Duncan and the Old Man who enters with Ross in act 2, scene 4. This is essentially a choral scene coming right after the murder of Duncan. The nameless Old Man is identified as being at least seventy by his opening line: "Three-score and ten I can remember well" (1). Like a chronicler of history, he speaks with the wisdom of age and experience. What has occurred is unnatural in a context of other weird and prodigious events that have recently taken place:

> On Tuesday last
> A falcon, tow'ring in her pride of place,
> Was by a mousing owl hawked at and killed. (11–13)

Ross also describes the strange and unprecedented behavior of Duncan's horses. These unnatural events register the perturbation in nature caused by the rightful king's murder.

Although Duncan only appears briefly in the play, he is clearly represented as an old man like Lear and Cymbeline. We are not given any indication how old he might be. We only have Lady Macbeth's surprising—and terrifying—lines: "Had he not resembled / My father as he slept, I had done't" (2.2.12–13). In her sleepwalking scene she again remembers the horrifying murder: "Yet who would have thought the old man to have had so much blood in him?" (5.1.42–43). Duncan is presented as a benevolent old man whose murder is especially cruel. He is a contextual figure and his murder overhangs the action. No one can ever forget him, especially Lady Macbeth in her madness. In the end, the despairing Macbeth will also be murdered. The wheel has come full circle.

3. TIME THE DESTROYER IN

THE *SONNETS* AND *THE RAPE OF LUCRECE*

Shakespeare's sonnets present a whole array of commonplaces about Time and its effects. These ideas frequently appeared in contemporary emblem books and their accompanying illustrations. Time's attributes are most often a scythe and/or sickle, an hourglass in which the sand trickles down, and a sundial clock. In terms of the seasons, spring and youth are linked, as are winter and death. Along with these conventional images, the tree that has lost its leaves is also an image of winter and approaching death. In the *Sonnets* Shakespeare is particularly fixated on wrinkles as a sign of old age and the loss of beauty, which can be subsumed under the theme of mutability and Time as a destroyer. As Shakespeare writes in Sonnet 65: "Since brass, nor stone, nor earth, nor boundless sea, / But sad mortality o'ersways their power." In this context "sad" means serious and grave, not sorrowful. Nothing can withstand "the wreckful siege of batt'ring days," not even "rocks impregnable" and "gates of steel." Time "decays" all, and nothing can "hold his swift foot back." Only the poem itself can withstand the ravages of

Time: "In black ink my love may still shine bright." This theme is repeated in quite a few of the sonnets. Although physical beauty may fade, the poem will survive. An even more common theme in the sonnets is that one's beauty will be perpetuated in one's children.

If one follows the usual ordering of the *Sonnets* as printed by Thomas Thorpe in 1609, Sonnet 2 comes as a bit of a surprise:

> When forty winters shall besiege thy brow,
> And dig deep trenches in thy beauty's field,
> Thy youth's proud livery, so gazed on now,
> Will be a tottered weed [tattered garment] of small worth held.

Shakespeare rarely mentions specific numbers, especially involving ages. Forty seems very early to be undergoing the ravages of time; one is reminded of his description of Cleopatra as "wrinkled deep in time" (*Antony and Cleopatra,* 1.5.29). "Deep trenches" are also an image of prominent wrinkles, which is Shakespeare's favorite image of old age in the *Sonnets.* "Youth's proud livery" is transformed into its opposite, "a tottered weed." The "treasure of thy lusty days" now lies "within thine own deep-sunken eyes." The persona of this sonnet seems remarkably old at forty. The only solution is to have a child: "This were to be new made when thou art old, / And see thy blood warm when thou feel'st it cold." Blood is the vehicle of sexual desire as well as one's inherited bloodline.

Sonnet 73 is the most successful representation of old age in relation to images of nature:

> That time of year thou mayst in me behold
> When yellow leaves, or none, or few, do hang
> Upon those boughs which shake against the cold,
> Bare ruined choirs where late the sweet birds sang.

The time of year is either autumn ("yellow leaves"), late autumn ("few"), or midwinter ("none"), although the boughs shaking against the cold suggest that it is winter. The editor of the Arden edition of the

Sonnets suggests that "in me" may refer to Shakespeare's own baldness, "hairless" being synonymous with "leafless."[1] (In *The Comedy of Errors* Dromio of Syracuse plays on this when he refers to "the plain bald pate of Father Time himself" [2.2.70–71].) The "bare ruined choirs" refers not only to the wintry trees that the songbirds formerly inhabited but also to the choirs of the disabused monasteries in which the church service was sung. The imagery deliberately maintains its double reference.

The next quatrain uses light imagery in the daily cycle as equivalents for the life span of man, where morning equals youth and night equals death:

> In me thou seest the twilight of such day
> As after sunset fadeth in the west,
> Which by and by black night doth take away,
> Death's second self, that seals up all in rest.

"Death's second self" usually means sleep, but here it also refers to night. (This is the only reference to "twilight" in Shakespeare.)

In the final quatrain fire serves as an image of life, just as ashes are an image of death:

> In me thou seest the glowing of such fire
> That on the ashes of his youth doth lie,
> As the deathbed whereon it must expire,
> Consumed with that which it was nourished by.

It is paradoxical that fire must consume the very substance that causes it to exist (Shakespeare uses the image of a burning candle to convey the same idea.) In this sonnet old age (and death) are represented by three familiar images: the tree that has lost its leaves, the fading of the light in the course of a natural day, and the fire that reduces everything to ashes and thus destroys itself.

A repeated theme in the *Sonnets* is that old age, which leads to death, destroys beauty. Looking in a mirror (or "glass") thus has negative connotations. The same holds true for the "dial" or sundial (although the image could also be that of a small clock or watch), which indicates the passage of time from youth to old age and death. Sonnet 77 opens with both of these images:

> Thy glass will show thee how thy beauties wear,
> Thy dial how thy precious minutes waste. . . .

The images are expanded in the second quatrain:

> The wrinkles which thy glass will truly show,
> Of mouthèd graves, will give thee memory;
> Thou by thy dial's shady stealth mayst know
> Time's thievish progress to eternity.

Here again Shakespeare is preoccupied with wrinkles, indicating encroaching old age. The wrinkles are deep and prominent, like a grave waiting to swallow a person up. Time is measured by the shadow the sundial casts, yet Time is a thief who moves by stealth toward death and eternity.

The poet imagines himself as very old compared to his love, who is in the bloom of youth. The disparities seem to be exaggerated for poetic effect. Sonnet 63 emphasizes the deep division between the two: "Against my love shall be as I am now, / With Time's injurious hand crushed and o'erworn." Here "against" means "in anticipation of the time when." Time is actively harmful—it is "injurious," crushing and wearing the poet down. At this moment "hours have drained his blood and filled his brow / With lines and wrinkles." Here again is the characteristic mark of old age, namely, wrinkles and lines in the face. His blood, the sign of youthful vigor, is now drained or thinned. In a conventional contrast between morning and night, the poet's

> youthful morn
> Hath traveled on to Age's steepy night,
> And all those beauties whereof now he's king

Are vanishing, or vanished out of sight,
Stealing away the treasure of his spring.

To defend "against confounding Age's cruel knife," the written poem will preserve the beauty both of the lover and his love. Thus, poetry guards against the ravages of time by extending into posterity.

Sonnet 60 begins with a wave breaking on the beach as a symbol of the cyclical (but not renewable) nature of time:

Like as the waves make towards the pebbled shore,
So do our minutes hasten to their end;
Each changing place with that which goes before,
In sequent toil all forwards do contend.

The forward motion of the waves is deceiving because they immediately reverse their motion. Birth ("Nativity") "crawls to maturity," as an infant crawls or an old man totters. Time is fickle, for what it once gave "doth now his gift confound"— presumably the gift of life. It is ultimately destructive:

Time doth transfix the flourish set on youth,
And delves the parallels in beauty's brow,
Feeds on the rarities of nature's truth,
And nothing stands but for his scythe to mow.

The "parallels in beauty's brow" are, of course, wrinkles. The "rarities" seem to represent natural wonders, as in the aspects of beauty. As in the "mower" poems of Andrew Marvell, Time is a mower whose scythe destroys all of creation indiscriminately.

Sonnet 100 also represents a protest against Time's destructive powers. The poet invokes his Muse to abandon "worthless song," redeem itself, and "my love's sweet face survey, / If Time have any wrinkle graven there." As Time writes on the face of the poet's love, so the poet's Muse engraves its own messages in the poem he is writing. The poet appeals to his Muse to "be a satire to decay / And make Time's spoils despisèd everywhere." "Satire" is presumably a satyr, the uncouth hairy being associated with the art of satire—very different from the poet's gracious Muse. The poet asks his Muse to endow his love with "fame faster than Time wastes life; / So thou prevent'st his scythe and crooked knife." To prevent something in Shakespeare's time was to undertake an action that would cause something not to happen. Thus, the poet's Muse is pitted against injurious Time, who destroys everything in sight with his scythe and crooked knife. The scythe or sickle *is* a crooked knife; the tautology makes the point emphatically.

The scythe is a frequent attribute of Time in the *Sonnets,* as in the closing couplet of Sonnet 12: "And nothing 'gainst Time's scythe can make defense, / Save breed, to brave him when he takes thee hence." Procreation as the way to defy Time in the early sonnets is matched by the written poem as an attempt at immortality in the later sonnets. Sonnet 12 presents conventional images of man's mortality:

> When I do count the clock that tells the time,
> And see the brave [splendid] day sunk in hideous night;
> When I behold the violet past prime,
> And sable [black] curls are silvered o'er with white.

Presumably a chiming clock is intended in the first line. Violets past their prime, or maturity, is an oft-repeated image of mutability in Shakespeare, as is the black hair that has turned white in the last line.

The next quatrain presents images of nature:

> When lofty trees I see barren of leaves,
> Which erst from heat did canopy the herd,
> And summer's green, all girded up in sheaves,
> Borne on the bier with white and bristly beard.

The trees providing shade for the cattle is a pastoral image. The green corn, bound up in sheaves, is now white and bristly as a result of drying, resembling an old man who, with "white and bristly beard," is dead and is being carried on his bier to his funeral. But beauty is vulnerable to Time's depradations because it "among the wastes of time must go." The process of decay is inevitable: "Since sweets and beauties do themselves forsake, / And die as fast as they see others grow." Time figures so prominently in the *Sonnets* because it represents mutability. Nothing can survive the progress of Time except procreation and the writing of poems.

In Sonnet 19 "Devouring Time" exercises its power among the mightiest. The poem represents an invocation to Time personified:

> blunt thou the lion's paws,
> And make the earth devour her own sweet brood;
> Pluck the keen teeth from the fierce tiger's jaws,
> And burn the long-lived phoenix in her blood.

The phoenix was a mythical bird reputed to live for five hundred years before being consumed in a fire it ignites itself. From its ashes it was then revived, thus renewing an eternal cycle. The poet here attributes to "Devouring Time" the unthinkable power to kill off the phoenix. He allows "swift-footed Time" to "do whate'er thou wilt . . . To the wide world and all her fading sweets." However, he sets forth one prohibition:

> O, carve not with thy hours my love's fair brow,
> Nor draw no lines there with thine antique pen.
> Him in thy course untainted do allow,
> For beauty's pattern to succeeding men.

Time's "antique pen" is both old and grotesque ("antic" being a variant spelling of "antique"). Time carves lines and wrinkles, while the poet's pen writes poems. Yet even if "old Time" (a familiar form of address) does its worst, the poet's love and his beauty will still live on in his verse.

Since most of the sonnets were written in the 1590s, it seems odd that Shakespeare, who was born in 1564, should represent the poet as very old. It's obvious that we in the twenty-first century have very different ideas about what it means to be old than Shakespeare's contemporaries did more than four hundred years ago. I have already mentioned Sonnet 2 ("When forty winters shall besiege thy brow"), yet there are constant reminders of the poet's old age throughout the *Sonnets*. For example, in Sonnet 62 the poet sees himself in his mirror as he really is, "beated and chopped with tanned antiquity." Here "beated" is a variant of "beaten" or battered, "chopped" is chapped or cracked, and "tanned antiquity" is a reference to the leathery skin of the very old. Yet the poet has lied about his appearance because he has been "painting my age with beauty of thy [his love's] days." Thus, the poet appropriates the youth and beauty of his love.

The point is made more directly in Sonnet 138, where the poet and his mistress participate in the same self-deception, namely, that he is young and that she is chaste:

Thus vainly thinking that she thinks me young,
Although she knows my days are past the best,
Simply I credit her false-speaking tongue;
On both sides thus is simple truth suppressed.

The sonnet is cynical and sophisticated:

But wherefore says she not she is unjust?
And wherefore say not I that I am old?
O, love's best habit is in seeming trust,
And age in love loves not t'have years told.

The aged lover doesn't want to be told that he is old and the unchaste mistress does not wish to be reminded of her infidelities. Love's best "habit" (or garment in its original sense) is not in establishing absolute truth but only in "seeming trust." The witty conclusion is an affirmation of an acceptable duplicity: "Therefore I lie with her, and she with me, / And in our faults by lies we flattered be." The wordplay refers to "lie" both in its sexual sense and its meaning of untruths.

In *The Rape of Lucrece* there is a lengthy invocation of Time personified by Lucrece. The images are familiar from the *Sonnets*, especially of Time the destroyer, who consumes youth and beauty. Lucrece begins by addressing Time, from whom she desires help in her grief:

> Misshapen Time, copesmate of ugly Night,
> Swift subtle post, carrier of grisly care,
> Eater of youth, false slave to false delight,
> Base watch of woes, sin's packhorse, virtue's snare! (925–28)

Time as the "eater of youth" is proverbial, deriving from the Latin tag *tempus edax rerum* (time that eats up all things), in Ovid's *Metamorphosis,* but truth is the daughter of time, as in the matching verbal tag *veritas, filia temporum.* The "watch" is a clock face on which woes are inscribed.

Time stamps "the seal of time in agèd things" (941), as if it were authenticating them, but it is primarily a destroyer: "To ruinate proud buildings with thy hours, / And smear with dust their glitt'ring golden tow'rs" (944–45). The "hours" of time indicate its progress. Among the other functions of time are the following:

> To fill with wormholes stately monuments,
> To feed oblivion with decay of things,
> To blot old books and alter their contents. (946–48)

The "stately monuments" are presumably made of wood. *The Rape of Lucrece* tends to accumulate and catalogue images of Time rather than present an argument, as in the *Sonnets.*

4. "HEAVY" FATHERS

Prospero in *The Tempest* is the prime example of a heavy or hard father in Shakespeare.[1] The character type owes a debt to the old man (*senex*) of Roman comedy, especially Plautus. In the latter's comedies he was generally wealthy and was strongly opposed to his son's interests, which were focused on raising the cash needed to buy the freedom of a beautiful young girl enslaved to a pimp and then to marry her. In the typical Plautean plot, the comic servant or parasite ingeniously persuades his master to fulfill his son's wishes. The machinery of Roman comedy was taken over by the Italian commedia dell'arte in the Renaissance. The Roman *senex* became the *pantalone* (or pantaloon) of Italian comedy. He is presented as an old man, rich and garrulous, who boasts of his sexual prowess (despite being thought impotent). Sometimes he pursues the same girl as his son. All these ideas are wonderfully displayed in Machiavelli's play *Mandragola* (ca. 1518).

Prospero is represented as an old man in *The Tempest*. Before being exiled twelve years ago, he was Duke of Milan. His daughter, Miranda, was then three years old, yet it seems much longer ago, for example, when he asks her what she sees "in the dark backward and abysm of time" (1.2.50). Following his "revels" speech at the end of the play, Prospero asks his prospective son-in-law, Ferdinand, to make allowances for the shortcomings of old age:

> Sir, I am vexed.
> Bear with my weakness; my old brain is troubled.
> Be not disturbed with my infirmity. (4.1.158–60)

In the final scene of the play Prospero seems to be preparing for death rather than an active career as Duke of Milan. Following the wedding of Ferdinand and Miranda, he says he will "retire me to my Milan, where / Every third thought shall be my grave" (5.1.311–12). This sounds very much like the end of *King Lear*.

Prospero is a heavy father in the way that he controls not only his daughter but also his spirit Ariel and his slave Caliban. In his role as a magician he exerts his power over everything. He has arranged to shipwreck Alonso, king of Naples, and the entire wedding party that attended the marriage of Alonso's daughter, Claribel, in Tunis. Yet he has also planned to shipwreck Ferdinand, the son of Alonso, in a different part of the island, where Prospero cunningly arranges for him to meet Miranda and fall in love with her. Prospero not only is a heavy father but also plays at being one, for example, in his pretended hostility toward Ferdinand, "lest too light winning / Make the prize light" (1.2.452–53). Every last detail of the marriage plot is worked out beforehand, with nothing left to chance. Ariel stages the shipwreck as a masquelike show and provides other spectacular presentations in the course of the play. At the end of the fourth act Prospero exults that "At this hour/ Lies at my mercy all mine enemies" (1.262–63).

In his first scene in the play Prospero informs his daughter about what has happened in the "dark backward and abysm of time" (1.2.50) and how he came to lose his dukedom. Yet he is very impatient with her, and, like an imperious schoolmaster, reminds her to listen carefully: "Ope thine ear. / Obey, and be attentive" (37–38). The audience becomes restive with Prospero's repetitions: "Dost thou attend me?" (78), "Thou attend'st not?" (87), "I pray thee mark me" (88), "Dost thou hear?" (106). Next he puts Miranda to sleep in order to take care of other business: "Thou art inclined to sleep. 'Tis a good dullness, / And give it way. I know thou canst not choose" (185–86). He wakes her up more than a hundred lines later (305).

Prospero controls every stage of Miranda's attraction to Ferdinand and their eventual betrothal. He treats her as if she were a small child, offering Ferdinand to her as his own personal gift: "The fringed curtains of thine eye advance / And say what thou seest yond" (1.2.409–10). Miranda thinks it is a spirit with a "brave form" (411), but Prospero assures her that Ferdinand is a human being. He is soon gloating to himself about his successful project, commenting in an aside: "It goes on, I see, / As my soul prompts it" (420–21). Later he is even more confident that the pair has fallen in love. In another aside he states: "At the first sight / They have changed eyes" (441–42). Next he arrests Ferdinand as a spy and puts him to work hauling logs. This is also a calculated move, as he reveals in yet another aside:

> They are both in either's pow'rs. But this swift business
> I must uneasy make, lest too light winning
> Make the prize light. (451–53)

This idea of deliberately putting obstacles in the path of the new lovers sounds very calculating, yet at this point Prospero is excessively purposive. He doesn't trust Miranda or Ferdinand to act on their natural impulses. At the end of the scene he congratulates himself on his magical skills, remarking: "It works" (495).

The fourth act continues the wooing of the first. Prospero offers Miranda to Ferdinand as his "gift" (4.1.13), although he warns him against the sin of lust in very moralistic terms:

> If thou dost break her virgin-knot before
> All sanctimonious ceremonies may
> With full and holy rite be minist'red,

No sweet aspersion shall the heavens let fall
To make this contract grow. (15–19)

Prospero sounds like Polonius lecturing Ophelia as if she were a baby:

Look thou be true. Do not give dalliance
Too much the rein; the strongest oaths are straw
To th' fire i' th' blood. Be more abstemious,
Or else good night your vow! (51–54)

Since Ferdinand always provides the right answers, one wonders why
Prospero is burdening him with all this heavy-handed moral advice.

Caliban is frequently referred to as Prospero's "slave" (1.2.308), as is
Ariel (270). If Prospero is a hard father to Miranda and to Ferdinand,
he is a slave master wielding an uncontested magic over Caliban. There
is no way for the surly Caliban to protest. Prosper is convinced that
he is

A devil, a born devil, on whose nature
Nurture can never stick; on whom my pains,
Humanely taken, all, all lost, quite lost! (4.1.188–90)

This is the part of the play that playwrights residing in the third world
are most eager to revise. Yet at the end Prospero admits that "this
thing of darkness I / Acknowledge mine" (5.1.275–76). Is this merely a
factual way to differentiate Caliban from Trinculo and Stephano, the
drunken sailors, or is Prospero acknowledging Caliban as his own
monstrous son? The passage is ambiguous on this point.

Lord Capulet in *Romeo and Juliet* is more literally a heavy or hard father than Prospero. Following the initial feud between the servants of
the Capulets and Montagues, the stage direction reads: *"Enter old Capulet in his gown, and his Wife"* (1.1.77). Presumably old Capulet has suddenly been roused from his sleep like Brabantio, Desdemona's father
(*Othello*, 1.1.156 s.d.). His warm dressing gown is typically worn by old

people. Capulet is clearly identified as an old man by his wife. He calls for his "long sword" (1.1.79), an old-fashioned, heavy weapon, but his wife has a more practical suggestion: "A crutch, a crutch! Why call you for a sword?" (79). Capulet, however, is aflame with the idea of vengeance: "My sword I say! Old Montague is come / And flourishes his blade in spite of me" (80–81). Whereupon old Montague enters with his wife. Prince Escalus is particularly perturbed by the fact that the feud has

> made Verona's ancient citizens
> Cast by their grave beseeming ornaments
> To wield old partisans, in hands as old,
> Cank'red with peace, to part your cank'red hate. (95–98)

It is worth noting how, right from the beginning, the feud is identified with the fateful doings of old men. The classic conflict between the young and the old prohibits any reconciliation and leads to the ensuing tragedy.

Before the ball at which Romeo first sees Juliet, Capulet is made to seem a witty and mellow old man, graciously acknowledging to his cousin that they are "past our dancing days" (1.5.33). When asked: "How long is't now since last yourself and I / Were in a mask?" (34–35)—presumably the mask was used at a costume ball—the cousin replies "thirty years" (35). Thus, Capulet must be well over fifty. His deep nostalgia about the past suggests that he is much older.

Capulet's rage in act 3, scene 5, comes as a surprise. This scene occurs after Romeo has killed Tybalt and been banished. Romeo and Juliet have been celebrating their lyrical marriage night when suddenly Juliet's mother informs her that, as compensation for her sorrowful mourning of her kinsmen Tybalt, her father has decided that she should be married to Paris right away. Old Capulet fully embodies the type of the patriarchal old father when he comes to announce his "decree" to Juliet (139). It is interesting that he uses the legal and political word "decree" to indicate that Juliet will have no part in his decision. He is genuinely surprised by his daughter's reaction:

How, how, how, how, chopped-logic? What is this?
"Proud"—and "I thank you"—and "I thank you not"—
And yet "not proud"? Mistress minion you,
Thank me no thankings, nor proud me no prouds,
But fettle your fine joints 'gainst Thursday next
To go with Paris to Saint Peter's Church,
Or I will drag thee on a hurdle thither. (150–56)

Capulet is genuinely enraged, seeming to curse his daughter as Lear curses Goneril and Regan:

My fingers itch. Wife, we scarce thought us blest
That God had lent us but this only child;
But now I see this one is one too much,
And that we have a curse in having her. (165–68)

The Nurse comforts Juliet, although she doesn't disagree with Capulet's decision, and Juliet suddenly finds herself completely alone.

At the end of the play the Capulets and the Montagues are both sorrowful about the tragic deaths their feud has wrought. Lady Capulet, who appeared to be about twenty-eight earlier in the play, says: "O me, this sight of death is as a bell / That warns my old age to a sepulcher" (5.3.206–7). This is a big contextual jump for Lady Capulet, who suddenly sees herself as an old lady. Montague offers to raise a statue to Juliet in pure gold, and Capulet responds for Romeo: "As rich shall Romeo's by his lady's lie— / Poor sacrifices of our enmity!" (303–4).

Capulet genuinely grieves when he discovers that his daughter is supposedly dead (she has drunk the sleeping potion provided by Friar Lawrence). He feels that his own life has ended, and he is prepared for death;

Death is my son-in-law, Death is my heir;
My daughter he hath wedded. I will die
And leave him all. Life, living, all is Death's. (4.5.38–40)

The ending of *Romeo and Juliet* is mournful. There is a sense that the young lovers are innocent victims of the feud, that they are not tragic protagonists at all but only "star-crossed lovers" (Prologue, 7).

Although Friar Lawrence is not a heavy father, he plays into the major themes of the play, so that by the end he is another sorrowful old man. At one point he clearly tells us that he is an old man. He refers to his "ancient ears" (2.3.74) and speaks about his troubled sleep: "Care keeps his watch in every old man's eye, / And where care lodges, sleep will never lie" (35–36). Although the inability to achieve restful sleep is most often associated with a guilty conscience (as in *Macbeth*), the melancholy young lovers paradoxically share this condition of sleeplessness with the elderly.

Right after the murder of Duncan, Macbeth thinks he hears a voice that cries

> "Sleep no more!
> Macbeth does murder sleep"—the innocent sleep,
> Sleep that knits up the raveled sleave of care,
> The death of each day's life, sore labor's bath,
> Balm of hurt minds, great nature's second course,
> Chief nourisher in life's feast—(2.2.34–39)

The same is also true of King Henry IV, who is troubled by a guilty conscience. In a long soliloquy he addresses sleep personified:

> O sleep, O gentle sleep,
> Nature's soft nurse, how have I frighted thee,
> That thou no more wilt weigh my eyelids down
> And steep my senses in forgetfulness? (*2 Henry IV,* 3.1.5–8)

Thus, sleeplessness links Friar Lawrence with Macbeth and Henry IV. The potion that he supplies Juliet is obviously well meant, but it all turns out tragically. One is reminded of Cordelia's dire expression of the irony of circumstance in *King Lear:* "We are not the first / Who with best meaning have incurred the worst" (5.3.3–4).

Two other heavy fathers who are curiously allied in their purposes are Egeus in *A Midsummer Night's Dream* and Brabantio in *Othello*. Both think their daughters have been overcome by magical charms. Right at the beginning of the play Egeus appears before Duke Theseus insisting that his daughter, Hermia, marry Demetrius and claiming that Lysander

> With cunning hast thou filched my daughter's heart,
> Turned her obedience, which is due to me,
> To stubborn harshness. (1.1.36–38)

As a patriarchal father, Egeus insists on "the ancient privilege of Athens" (41):

> As she is mine, I may dispose of her,
> Which shall be either to this gentleman [Demetrius]
> Or to her death, according to our law. (42–44)

The duke, however, modifies the decree and offers poor Hermia a better choice:

> Either to die the death, or to abjure
> Forever the society of men.
> Therefore, fair Hermia, question your desires;
> Know of your youth, examine well your blood [the seat of
>   desire],
> Whether, if you yield not to your father's choice,
> You can endure the livery of a nun. (65–70)

Hermia, of course, has no real choice and flees Athens together with Lysander.

In *Othello* Brabantio is represented as an old man. Like Lord Capulet in *Romeo and Juliet*, his sleep is broken by the crude accusations of Iago and Roderigo that "an old black ram / Is tupping your white ewe"

(85–86)—in other words, that Othello has eloped with Desdemona, Brabantio's daughter. He enters in his "nightgown," or dressing gown, and immediately goes before the Venetian senate to accuse Othello. In the encounter in the next scene Othello wisely suggests: "Good signior, you shall more command with years / Than with your weapons" (1.2.59–60). Undaunted, Brabantio accuses Othello of using magical potions to win Desdemona:

> I therefore vouch again
> That with some mixtures pow'rful o'er the blood,
> Or with some dram, conjured to this effect,
> He wrought upon her. (1.3.103–6)

Othello protests his innocence, but it is the speech of Desdemona that convinces her father that there is no possibility of intervention.

It is interesting that Othello attests to his friendship with Brabantio: "Her father loved me; oft invited me" (1.3.127). There are some xenophobic and racist sentiments lurking in Brabantio's mind, and he expresses his disappointment that his daughter should shun "the wealthy, curlèd darlings of our nation" (1.2.67). Brabantio's heart is broken. At the end of the play, Gratiano announces his death following Othello's murder of Desdemona:

> Poor Desdemon! I am glad thy father's dead.
> Thy match was mortal to him, and pure grief
> Shore his old thread in twain. (5.2.201–3)

Although in *A Midsummer Night's Dream* all the perturbations are resolved in a happy ending, this is not the case in the tragic outcome of *Othello*.

Shylock in *The Merchant of Venice* is another hard father. He refers to himself as "old Shylock" (2.5.2) and Bassanio speaks of him as Launcelot's "old master" (2.2.152). In act 2, scene 5, Shylock is bid forth to supper. Leaving his keys with Jessica, he gives her very explicit instructions:

Lock up my doors; and when you hear the drum
And the vile squealing of the wry-necked fife,
Clamber not you up to the casements then,
Nor thrust your head into the public street
To gaze on Christian fools with varnished faces. (29–33)

This sounds like Voltore's instructions to his wife in Ben Jonson's *Volpone* (1606). Shylock is a controlling figure throughout the play. Before he leaves, he insists on yet another word of caution for Jessica:

Do as I bid you, shut doors after you.
Fast bind, fast find,
A proverb never stale in thrifty mind. (52–54)

Jessica, however, has other ideas: "Farewell; and if my fortune be not crost, / I have a father, you a daughter, lost" (55–56). She plans to elope with Lorenzo and abscond with her father's money and jewels. Unlike Prospero, Shylock never expresses one kind word to his daughter.

It is unfortunate that Jessica as a character is not more fully developed, but her departure and conversion to Christianity enrage Shylock, and the action becomes more dire. Like all the preceding heavy fathers, Shylock cannot understand Jessica's departure: "My own flesh and blood to rebel!" (3.1.32). And again: "I say my daughter is my flesh and my blood" (35). Shylock is conflicted between love for his daughter and love of his money and jewels: "I would my daughter were dead at my foot, and the jewels in her ear! Would she were hearsed at my foot, and the ducats in her coffin" (83–84). What enrages him the most is that Jessica has traded the turquoise ring that his late wife had given him for a monkey: "Out upon her! Thou torturest me, Tubal. It was my turquoise; I had it of Leah when I was a bachelor. I would not have given it for a wilderness of monkeys" (113–16). It is unclear whether Shylock thinks that his daughter is unthrify and has traded a valuable turquoise ring for a mere monkey or whether he is infuriated at her alienation from him. When she becomes a Christian, she does not retain any remembrance of having been a Jewess.

In the trial scene (4.1) Shylock once again remembers his daughter after Portia has entered and he is ready to cut off his pound of Bassanio's flesh:

These be the Christian husbands! I have a daughter:
Would any of the stock of Barabbas
Had been her husband, rather than a Christian! (294–96)

Barabbas is an obvious reference to the protagonist of Marlowe's play *The Jew of Malta* (1592). Shylock may still be thinking about his daughter, but she is clearly not thinking about him. She says: "I am never merry when I hear sweet music" (5.1.69), but her melancholy does not include thoughts of the Jewish father she has so unthinkingly abandoned.

Although Northumberland is not a hard father, like old Capulet or Egeus, his desertion of his son, Hotspur, in battle is notable. He is always realigning himself with the winning side, as in *Richard II*, where he becomes Bolingbroke's trusted lieutenant. In his deposition Richard reveals his political opportunism: "Northumberland, thou ladder wherewithal / The mounting Bolingbroke ascends my throne" (5.1.55–56). Richard predicts that Northumberland will change sides again, which he does when he joins the conspiracy against Bolingbroke (now King Henry IV) in *1 Henry IV*. Richard characterizes him as an unstable, self-important person who is not to be trusted.

In *1 Henry IV* Northumberland is unable to send his forces to join the rebels fighting against the king. Although he claims that he is sick, his son is not convinced:

Sick now? Droop now? This sickness doth infect
The very lifeblood of our enterprise.
'Tis catching hither, even to our camp. (4.1.28–30)

There are so many provisos in Northumberland's letter that it is not very convincing. Hotspur's death in act 5, scene 4, is directly contingent on his father's absence. In the Induction to *2 Henry IV*, Rumor, *"painted full of tongues,"* tells us clearly that old Northumberland in his castle "lies crafty-sick" (37). He is feigning sickness to avoid the field of battle, where his son has been killed.

Although much is made of the death of Hotspur, Northumberland appears emotionally aloof. He jests wittily on his son's name:

> Ha? Again.
> Said he young Harry Percy's spur was cold?
> Of Hotspur Coldspur? That rebellion
> Had met ill luck? (1.1.48–51)

Northumberland's pun on Hotspur's death—he is now Coldspur—seems highly inappropriate in this context. There is no evidence of mourning for his dead son.

The rebels greatly depend on Northumberland's forces: "Our supplies live largely in the hope / Of great Northumberland" (1.3.12–13). The death of Hotspur, the result of his father not coming to his aid, is clearly on everyone's mind. Lord Bardolph explicitly states that Hotspur

> lined himself with hope,
> Eating the air and promise of supply,
> Flatt'ring himself in project of a power
> Much smaller than the smallest of his thoughts,
> And so, with great imagination
> Proper to madmen, led his powers to death
> And, winking, leaped into destruction. (27–33)

No one can forget Northumberland's abandonment of his own son in battle.

The theme reaches its climax in act 2, scene 3. Northumberland is again hesitant to go into battle. Hotspur's widow, Lady Percy, reminds him of his betrayal:

> The time was, father, that you broke your word,
> When you were more endeared to it than now,

When your own Percy, when my heart's dear Harry,
Threw many a northward look to see his father
Bring up his powers, but he did long in vain. (10–14)

Lady Percy presents an extremely moving eulogy for the death of
Hotspur, which repeatedly refers to Northumberland's slackness:

> Him did you leave,
> Second to none, unseconded by you,
> To look upon the hideous god of war
> In disadvantage, to abide a field
> Where nothing but the sound of Hotspur's name
> Did seem defensible. So you left him. (33–38)

True to character, Northumberland does not join the rebel forces, who
are waiting for him, instead choosing to flee to Scotland.

5. POLITIC OLD MEN:

POLONIUS, NESTOR, AND MENENIUS

Shakespeare reveals an interest in developing the character of politic old men like Polonius in *Hamlet*, Nestor in *Troilus and Cressida*, and Menenius in *Coriolanus*. By "politic" I mean someone who is interested in politics and government, although the word also has the negative connotation of "Machiavellian" or crafty; in other words, using politics or "policy" for personal gain. All three of these characters are old men who have acquired wisdom from long experience. They are skillful rhetoricians and orators, yet they are also unscrupulous in their moral commitments. As was previously mentioned, Shakespeare is fascinated by the type of the *senex* from Roman comedy, which he develops in the many heavy fathers in his works. If you pursue the type further, one characteristic of the *senex*—and of old men in general—is that they tend to be garrulous and long-winded.

This is best illustrated by Polonius. As represented in many theatrical productions, he comes across as a foolish, talkative old man, yet he is also very important politically. He is the king's chief counselor, and it seems fairly obvious that he has helped Claudius to ascend the throne. One has the impression that Polonius is just on the point of having outlived his usefulness. He has become superannuated. Shakespeare expends a great deal of effort to represent this stylistically. Polonius is clearly an unstoppable talker and rhetorician, a "foolish prating knave" (3.4.216), as Hamlet calls him after he has accidentally murdered him. "Prate" is a particularly apt word to describe him, meaning to talk idly and foolishly and not to the point. Later an angry Hamlet uses the word to challenge a boastful Laertes at his sister's grave: "And if thou prate of mountains, let them throw / Millions of acres on us" (5.1.282–83). This is part of Laertes' overwrought discourse, which Hamlet vows to match: "I'll rant as well as thou" (286). Significantly, in *Coriolanus* "prate" is used by the protagonist as a contemptuous term associated with the plebeians. Right before he is banished, Coriolanus throws the term back at the tribunes: "What do you prate of service?" (3.3.83). "Prate" also implies talk without any basis in reality. In her embassy to her son to spare Rome, Volumnia fears that all her talk is useless:

> There's no man in the world
> More bound to's mother, yet here he lets me prate
> Like one i' th' stocks. (5.3.158–60)

"Prate" here implies purposeless, pointless talk—mere chatter.

In *Hamlet* Shakespeare presents Polonius as an extreme example of the *senex* type. He is not only old and long-winded but also frequently shown losing the thread of the conversation. There is thus the implication of cognitive impairment and senility. Of course, this is only an implication, and throughout most of the play Polonius is cunning and courtly. For example, in an otherwise not very important scene between Polonius and his servant, Reynaldo, Polonius is providing him with careful instructions concerning how to spy on his son in Paris. He suggests that Reynaldo first ingratiate himself with Laertes' friends and then invent faults in Laertes' character—gaming, drinking, fencing, swearing, quarreling, whoring—to draw his friends out. Polonius boasts of his skill in policy or statecraft:

> And thus do we of wisdom and of reach,
> With windlasses and with assays of bias,
> By indirections find directions out. (2.1.64–66)

"Bias" is the curved course of a bowling alley, where the bowling ball cannot be thrown straight.

In this seemingly pointless scene, which doesn't have any bearing on the main action, there is a very significant moment when Polonius loses the thread of his discourse. This happens rarely in Shakespeare, and it is used here to make a very definite point about the character of Polonius. He rambles on to Reynaldo about how clever his scheme is—"a fetch of warrant" (38)—to lay "slight sullies" (39) on his son in the hope that the person Reynaldo is talking to will answer with his own contributions. Polonius then conjures up that person's hypothetical reply:

> He closes with you in this consequence
> "Good sir," or so, or "friend," or "gentleman"—
> According to the phrase or the addition
> Of man and country— (45–48)

It is in this thicket of pointless verbiage that Polonius gets completely lost:

> And then, sir, does 'a this—'a does—
> What was I about to say? By the mass, I was about to say
>   something!
> Where did I leave? (49–51)

Reynaldo politely tries to get his master back on track, and Polonius returns to "closes in the consequence" (54). I find this scene a remarkable piece of writing in the colloquial idiom. It sets the stage for everything we think about Polonius in the balance of the play.

In the first long scene with Polonius we already see that he displays many of the characteristics of the *senex*. When his son leaves for Paris, he offers him "these few precepts" (1.3.58), which are not few in number at all but consist of a long list of moral apothegms that are all clichés. For example:

> Costly thy habit as thy purse can buy,
> But not expressed in fancy; rich, not gaudy,
> For the apparel oft proclaims the man. (70–72)

Who could disagree with that advice? Laertes is usually portrayed as impatient with his father's wise saws and eager to depart. Even Polonius's oft-quoted conclusion is a moralistic truism that doesn't say much:

> This above all, to thine own self be true,
> And it must follow, as the night the day,
> Thou canst not then be false to any man. (78–80)

Laertes is not a child, and these bromides are not very helpful to him.

Polonius then turns to Ophelia and forces her to reveal her conversation with her recently departed brother. Ophelia is an innocent and inexperienced young girl whose confession in this scene bodes ill for her ultimate fate in the play: "I do not know, my lord, what I should think" (104), to which her father replies emphatically: "Marry, I will teach you. Think yourself a baby" (105). Polonius speaks like an old father cynical in the world's ways, as Prospero is in *The Tempest*. Ophelia thinks that Hamlet has importuned her "with love / In honorable fashion" (110–11), but to her father these are only

> springes to catch woodcocks [a stupid bird]. I do know
> When the blood burns, how prodigal the soul
> Lends the tongue vows. (115–17)

In a later scene Polonius, in conversation with Hamlet, claims to have once been a lover who, he firmly believes, has gone mad from thwarted love for his daughter: "And truly in my youth I suffered much extremity for love" (2.2.190–92). Ophelia is cowed into submission (as her brother isn't), and she ends the scene with: "I shall obey, my lord" (1.3.136). By act 2, scene 1, Polonius is absolutely convinced of Hamlet's mad love of Ophelia. He congratulates himself on his correct but perhaps overcalculating shrewdness characteristic of an old man:

> By heaven, it is as proper to our age
> To cast beyond ourselves in our opinions
> As it is common for the younger sort
> To lack discretion. (114–17)

He doesn't think much of the reasoning powers of young people like his son and daughter.

In the next scene he appears before the king and queen full of self-congratulation that he has found the cause of Hamlet's madness. He preens with self-importance and insists that the king should first admit the ambassadors from Norway, at which point "my news shall be the fruit to that great feast" (2.2.52). Shakespeare goes to great pains to write a parodistic rhetorical oration for Polonius, like the parody of fancy rhetoric and diction spoken by Osric in act 5, scene 2. Polonius has studied his speech carefully, to the point where it almost sounds memorized. It has a very formal introduction, which doesn't get to the point for quite a few lines. It is quoted it at length to give the reader some idea of its rhetorical expansiveness:

> My liege and madam, to expostulate
> What majesty should be, what duty is,
> Why day is day, night night, and time is time,
> Were nothing but to waste night, day, and time.
> Therefore, since brevity is the soul of wit,
> And tediousness the limbs and outward flourishes,
> I will be brief. Your noble son is mad. (86–92)

Although the speech is comprised of inanities, it is a well-turned and sonorous rhetorical period, complicated in its mastery of courtly diction.

There is an immediate, implicit criticism when the queen says, "More matter, with less art," but Polonius swears that he "uses no art at all" (95–96). Art, of course, is the art of rhetoric as opposed to plain speaking. Once started, Polonius cannot be dissuaded from delivering his prepared oration. With extraordinary art he swears that he uses no art at all, in other words, that he speaks directly and to the point:

> That he's mad, 'tis true: 'tis true 'tis pity,
> And pity 'tis 'tis true—a foolish figure.
> But farewell it, for I will use no art. (97–99)

The "figure" refers to the art of rhetoric discussed in the many elaborate treatises of Shakespeare's time.

In reading Hamlet's badly conceived love letter to Ophelia, Polonius shows himself to be something of a literary critic. He objects to Hamlet's salutation to "the most beautified Ophelia"—"That's an ill phrase, a vile phrase; 'beautified' is a vile phrase" (111–12). Of course, "beautified" suggests that Ophelia is not naturally beautiful but relies on cosmetics, the "plast'ring art," like the "harlot's cheek" in the king's confessional aside (3.1.51). Polonius also comments decisively on the Player's Dido and Aeneas speech, insisting "this is too long" (2.2.509), but Hamlet objects. When Hamlet questions the odd phrase "mobled [muffled] queen," Polonius jumps in with his conclusive "That's good. 'Mobled queen' is good" (515). Is it good or is it part of the archaized diction of the Player's speech? Polonius also tells us that he once was a thespian in the university and was "accounted a good actor" (3.2.103–4). He played Julius Caesar and "was killed i' th' Capitol; Brutus killed me" (105–6). Hamlet can't resist the obvious pun: "It was a brute part of him to kill so capital a calf there" (107–8). This casual exchange foreshadows the death of Polonius in act 3, scene 4.

As the play progresses, Polonius sticks to his conviction that Hamlet is mad for Ophelia's love. Claudius and Gertrude are increasingly skeptical, but they allow Polonius to prove his point. This involves various cruel and secretive maneuvers. In one scene Polonius sets up Ophelia with a prayer book to trap Hamlet into confessing, but even he, the master politician, is aware (in an aside) that there is something wrong with his underhanded scenario:

> We are oft to blame in this,
> 'Tis too much proved, that with devotion's visage
> And pious action we do sugar o'er
> The devil himself. (3.1.46–49)

This immediately triggers the King's confessional aside.

In preparation for Hamlet's scene with his mother, Polonius is up to his usual tricks: "Behind the arras I'll convey myself / To hear the process" (3.3.28–29). In the closet scene, when Gertrude fears that Hamlet is about to murder her, Polonius cries out "What, ho! Help!" (24) from behind the arras. Whereupon he is immediately stabbed by Hamlet: "How now? A rat? Dead for a ducat, dead!" (25). Hamlet's disdain for Polonius permeates the scene. When he lifts the arras and sees him, he remarks contemptuously: "Thou wretched, rash, intruding fool, farewell! / I took thee for thy better" (32–33), namely, the king.

At the end of the scene Hamlet shows no grief for the departed counselor: "I'll lug the guts into the neighbor room" (213). His final words are dismissive:

> Indeed, this counselor
> Is now most still, most secret, and most grave,
> Who was in life a foolish prating knave. (214–16)

Hamlet can't seem to forgive Polonius for his tedious and long-winded rhetoric. Polonius represents old-fashioned political and personal values. He is cunning and devious and will do anything to achieve his objectives. Hamlet satirically applauds the fact that Polonius is now "most still" (he has no more oratorical flourishes), "most secret" (in his plotting he has quietly slipped into his own death), and "most grave"(with a bitter pun on gravity of demeanor and the grave in which he will ultimately rest).

The Ghost of Hamlet's father is definitely conceived as old rather than tedious, yet a spirit that nevertheless talks at length. Following the stage direction *"Ghost cries under the stage"* (1.5.148), Hamlet addresses it jocularly as if it were a diabolical spirit: "Well said, old mole! Canst work i' th' earth so fast? / A worthy pioner!" (162–63). The image is that of a digger or miner in the earth, like a burrowing mole. Hamlet addresses the Ghost with excessive familiarity: "Ha, ha, boy, say'st thou so? Art thou there, truepenny?" (150). "Truepenny" means an honest fellow. How to explain Hamlet's irreverence at this point? As Horatio concludes, these are clearly part of his "wild and whirling words" (133).

Parallel to the Ghost is the figure of the Player King in the "Mousetrap" play-within-a-play, who is meant to stand in for Hamlet's father. Both the Player King and the Player Queen are represented as old. In his first speech the Player King makes it abundantly evident that they have been married for thirty years:

> Full thirty times hath Phoebus' cart [the sun's chariot] gone round
> Neptune's salt wash and Tellus' orbèd ground.
> And thirty dozen moons with borrowed sheen
> About the world have times twelve thirties been,
> Since love our hearts, and Hymen did our hands,
> Unite commutual in most sacred bands. (3.2.159–64)

If they have been married for thirty years, the Player King and Queen must be at least fifty but probably much older. Thus their ages bear directly on those of Hamlet's mother and father in the play.

Shakespeare goes to a lot of trouble to make the Player King and Queen speak in a stilted and archaized style. They are figures from the olden times. Their end-stopped heroic couplets are not only very old-fashioned but are also very circumlocutory. That makes the Player King sound like Polonius and thus a member of the circle of long-winded, tedious old men. Shakespeare seems to be enjoying himself by making the Player King speak in formal perorations rather than in colloquial speech, which would have been easier to write. The enjoyment may derive from writing against the grain in tedious and ponderous formal speech—a technical rhetorical achievement. Other plays-within-a-play are similarly archaized—for example the "Nine Worthies" in *Love's Labor's Lost* and "Pyramus and Thisby" in *A Midsummer Night's Dream*.

In Aeneas's tale to Dido that Hamlet begins and the Player continues, the figures of old Priam and Hecuba are similarly archaized. These speeches are written in a high-flown, rhetorical style with a very Latinate, polysyllabic diction. For example, the "hellish Pyrrhus" (2.2.474) is "o'ersizèd with coagulate gore" (473). This is the only use of "o'ersized" in all of Shakespeare. "Size" is a kind of glue, and Pyrrhus is

> horridly tricked
> With blood of fathers, mothers, daughters, sons,
> Baked and impasted with the parching streets. (468–70)

Pyrrhus is a static, seemingly painted figure of the Avenger. "Old grandsire Priam" (475) in Homer's *Iliad* is a type figure of the old man (as is Aeneas's father, Anchises, in Virgil's *Aeneid*). Priam fits in with other old men in the play, like old Hamlet and old Norway. "His antique sword" (480) is useless, "Rebellious to his arm" (481). He is the "unnervèd father" (485), weak and feeble in sinew (the first recorded use of "unnervèd"). He is called the "reverend Priam" (490), an old man worthy of reverence, and Pyrrhus's sword is declining on his "milky head" (489), presumably his white hair, an identifying mark of an old man.

Troilus and Cressida has more old men than any other Shakespeare play. There is a particular emphasis on Nestor, the old man in Homer's *Iliad*. Ulysses refers to him as "most reverend for thy stretched-out life" (1.3.61). "Reverend" means worthy of respect, and it is often used in Shakespeare for old men. Hector uses it flatteringly for Nestor in the following passage:

Let me embrace thee, good old chronicle,
That hast so long walked hand in hand with time.
Most reverend Nestor, I am glad to clasp thee. (4.5.201–3)

In an effort to get Coriolanus chosen for consul, Menenius politely addresses the patricians and tribunes as "Most reverend and grave elders" (*Coriolanus,* 2.2.43). "Reverend" and "reverence" are terms particularly associated with the old and reflect the respect due them because of their age. As Goneril ironically says to Lear: "As you are old and reverend, should be wise" (*King Lear,* 1.4.231).

Nestor is generally represented positively. Ulysses refers to him as "venerable Nestor, hatched in silver" (1.3.65). His gray hair is a conventional sign of old age. Ulysses goes out of his way to praise him, although he doesn't necessarily agree with his counsel. Nestor is "instructed by the antiquary times, / He must, he is, he cannot but be wise" (2.3.252–53). It's hard to know whether the wily Ulysses is dismissing Nestor with conventional, fulsome praise.

Yet there is also a negative aspect to the representation of the old and reverend Nestor. The scurrilous but usually truthful Thersites calls him "that stale old mouse-eaten dry cheese" (5.4.10–11), and, earlier he is referred to as "old Nestor, whose wit was moldy ere your grandsires had nails on their toes" (2.1.108–10). This is an odd reference to Nestor, as if he is long past being superannuated. He does say to Hector: "I knew thy grandsire, / And once fought with him" (4.5.195–96). How old, then, is Nestor? He seems well past Lear's four score and upward. When the Greek generals line up to kiss the newly arrived Cressida, Nestor is the first in line, after which Achilles says: "I'll take that winter from your lips, fair lady" (4.5.24), an obvious reference to the coldness of Nestor's kiss. According to the theory of the humors, old men were cold and dry in temperament. They needed the proper food and drink to warm them up. In Ulysses' account of Patroclus's imitation of old Nestor, he has all the physical defects traditionally attributed to old age. When Patroclus mimes the old man arming to answer a night alarm, he presents a ridiculous figure unsuitable for military action:

the faint defects of age
Must be the scene of mirth; to cough and spit,
And with a palsy fumbling on his gorget,
Shake in and out the rivet. (1.3.172–75)

Like Polonius, Nestor is an ambiguous figure. He is long-winded and garrulous and sometimes loses the thread of his discourse, as in his speech to Hector:

Ha,
By this white beard, I'd fight with thee tomorrow.
Well, welcome, welcome. I have seen the time— (4.5.207–9)

Ulysses immediately cuts him off before he can venture into a long, nostalgic discourse about times past. This suggests that the wily Ulysses finds Nestor tedious.

Nestor is a classic archetype of the wise old man, an orator and distinguished speaker about whom there are many casual references in Shakespeare's works. Besides *Troilus and Cressida*, perhaps the most extended discussion of Nestor is in Shakespeare's early narrative poem *The Rape of Lucrece*. Lucrece's extended description of the Troy painting (or painted tapestry), drawn from Virgil's *Aeneid*, includes several stanzas about Nestor, of which this is the first:

There pleading might you see grave Nestor stand,
As 'twere encouraging the Greeks to fight,
Making such sober action with his hand
That it beguiled attention, charmed the sight.
In speech it seemed his beard, all silver white,
    Wagged up and down, and from his lips did fly
    Thin winding breath which purled up to the sky. (1401–7)

Here Nestor is clearly represented as a dignified old orator.

Another old man in *Troilus and Cressida* is Pandarus, the uncle of Cressida, who panders his niece to Troilus. Again, Pandarus does much to dampen and qualify Troilus's youthful, romantic ardor. At the end of act 1, scene 1, Troilus complains:

> I cannot come to Cressid but by Pandar;
> And he's as tetchy to be wooed to woo
> As she is stubborn, chaste, against all suit. (99–101)

The term "tetchy" means peevish, touchy, irritable. At the end of the play Pandarus is sick: "A whoreson tisick, a whoreson rascally tisick so troubles me" (5.3.101–2). "Tisick" is our modern "phthisic," a consumptive cough, but the suggestion is that it is something more serious since Pandarus thinks that he will soon die. He is also suffering from "a rheum in mine eyes too, and such an ache in my bones that, unless a man were cursed, I cannot tell what to think on't" (5.3.104–7). Aching bones is, of course, a symptom of venereal disease and not necessarily a malady of old age. This is the subject of Pandarus's epilogue, addressed to "good traders in the flesh" (5.10.46), who might be in the audience. He has advice for "brethren and sisters of the hold-door trade" (51) since he believes he has only two more months to live. His concluding couplet is appropriate for his scurrilous role: "Till then I'll sweat and seek about for eases, / And at that time bequeath you my diseases" (55–56). The sweating tub was the usual treatment for venereal disease, the "Neapolitan bone-ache" (2.3.19) that Thersites speaks of. At the end of the play Pandarus seems old and decrepit—and not just because he suffers from venereal disease.

Like Polonius and Nestor, Menenius in *Coriolanus* is politic.[1] Along with Volumnia, Coriolanus's mother, he serves as the chief spokesman for the patriarchal, aristocratic values of Rome. He is clearly contemptuous of the plebeians and their tribunes, yet he is also clever and witty in his discourse, so that he can give the impression that he is practical and willing to compromise. The opening stage direction reveals a serious threat: *"Enter a company of mutinous Citizens, with staves, clubs, and other weapons"* (1.1). This scene is definitely related to the food riots that were taking place in London at the time. The First Citizen announces that "Caius Marcius [later called Coriolanus] is chief enemy to the people" (7–8). Menenius enters and tries to calm the popular insurrection. His "pretty tale" (91) of the Belly and the Members tries to show that Rome consists of a harmonious community of patricians and plebeians. However, it is all a thinly disguised attempt to conceal the patricians' arbitrary power and doesn't address the plebeians' argument that grain is wildly overpriced and that they are hungry.

The whole scene is a good example of Menenius's wit and his skill at purely political rhetoric. He is a master of the colloquial style, which tries not to offend anyone. His tale—based on contemporary political writings—is presented as a fable, with the Belly representing the patricians and the Members the plebeians. In his concluding remarks Menenius simplifies the political allegory:

> The senators of Rome are this good Belly,
> And you the mutinous members. For examine
> Their counsels and their cares, disgest [digest] things rightly
> Touching the weal o' th' common, you shall find
> No public benefit which you receive
> But it proceeds or comes from them to you,
> And no way from yourselves. (149–55)

The argument, of course, is specious yet nevertheless effective. Menenius is rather long-winded in his elaborate parallels, and the First Citizen is conscious of the tediousness: "Y'are long about it" (128).

Menenius is equally effective in speaking with the tribunes about the plebeians. He is a rhetorician, pure and simple, and it hardly matters whether what he is saying is true or morally justified. All he desires is to be persuasive. He characterizes himself as a "humorous patrician, and one that loves a cup of hot wine with not a drop of allaying Tiber [water from the Tiber] in't" (2.1.47–49). He shamelessly insults the tribunes while seeming to flatter them. He represents himself as frank above all: "What I think I utter, and spend my malice in my breath" (53–54). This is not true, of course, since he is wily and crafty. He seems to entangle the tribunes in a web of words, so that it is difficult to untangle what he is really saying. For example, referring to the characterization he has just given of himself, he asks: "What harm can your bisson conspectuities glean out of this character"? (65–66). "Bisson," an odd word with an archaic flavor meaning "blind," occurs only once in the histrionic Player's speech in *Hamlet,* when he is speaking of the distraught Queen Hecuba, running "barefoot up and down, threat'ning the flames [of burning Troy] / With bison rheum" (2.2.516–17). "Bisson rheum" are blinding tears. "Conspectuities" is a Shakespearean coinage for the visual powers. It looks as if Menenius is trying to dazzle the slow-witted tribunes with his flamboyant patrician style.

Menenius plays a role similar to Volumnia's in trying to calm Coriolanus and teach him to dissemble his aristocratic petulance in order to be chosen consul. Here we see Menenius in the familiar role as mediator:

I'll try whether my old wit be in request
With those that have but little. This must be patched
With cloth of any color. (3.1.250–52)

Coriolanus may be "too absolute" (3.2.39), but Menenius and Volumnia are wheelers and dealers who will do whatever it takes to achieve their political goals. In this scene Menenius once again resorts to the bodily imagery of the fable. Coriolanus is "a limb that has but a disease; / Mortal, to cut it off; to cure it, easy" (3.1.294–95). And again:

The service of the foot
Being once gangrened, is not then respected
For what before it was. (304–6)

The reasoning is as specious here as it was in the first scene of the play. One has to admire Coriolanus for maintaining his own honesty.

When Coriolanus departs Rome to go into exile, we are acutely aware that Menenius is an old man. At the end of the scene he says:

If I could shake off but one seven years
From these old arms and legs, by the good gods,
I'd with thee every foot. (4.1.55–57)

In Menenius' unsuccessful embassy to beg Coriolanus not to attack Rome, we feel that he has lost his political power and is now a broken old man. He pleads with Coriolanus to relent:

> The glorious gods sit in hourly synod about thy particular prosperity, and love thee no worse than thy old father Menenius does! O my son, my son! Thou art preparing fire for us; look thee, here's water [tears] to quench it. (5.2.69–73)

It is interesting that Menenius, as surrogate father of Coriolanus, fails where Volumnia, his mother, succeeds. The rejection of Menenius is like the rejection of Falstaff by Prince Hal, now King Henry V, in *2 Henry IV*.

6. WISE OLD MEN

After the protagonist in *Timon of Athens* has died, a soldier finds Timon's grave but cannot read the inscription. He makes a wax impression, which he will take to his captain, who "hath in every figure skill, / An aged interpreter, though young in days" (5.3.8–9). "Aged" means experienced, but it can also mean wise in this context. The young captain is presumably wise beyond his years. If old men often carry negative connotations in Shakespeare, a number of almost ideal, wise old men speak to us out of their rich and varied experience. This is a traditional and biblical view of old men as sages and reverend counselors.

The banished Duke Senior in *As You Like It* is presented as one of these wise old men.[1] He lives in pastoral exile in the Forest of Arden as if he were still in the Golden Age. His "philosophy" seems to be expressed in the following statement:

Sweet are the uses of adversity,
Which, like the toad, ugly and venomous,
Wears yet a precious jewel in his head. (2.1.12–14)

He contrasts the tranquil sweetness of life in the forest with the "painted pomp" (3) at "the envious court" (4). In the forest Duke Senior and his "co-mates and brothers in exile" (1) have escaped from "the penalty of Adam" (5), or original sin. They are like Polixenes and Leontes in *The Winter's Tale*, playing like "twinned lambs, that did frisk i' th' sun" (1.2.67), who "knew not / The doctrine of ill-doing, nor dreamed / That any did" (69–71). The life of Duke Senior and his co-mates has a sacramental quality. It "finds tongues in trees, books in the running brooks, / Sermons in stones, and good in everything" (2.1.16–17).

Duke Senior is not a very well developed character, but old Adam, the loyal and generous servant of Orlando, is more fully presented as another wise old man. He is, by his own admission, "almost fourscore" (2.3.71)—a little younger than King Lear—and he is represented as an ideal type of the devoted servant. Orlando speaks an encomium for him:

O good old man, how well in thee appears
The constant [faithful] service of the antique world,
When service sweat for duty, not for meed [recompense]!
    (56–58)

Adam is not only old but old-fashioned, and he lauds the virtues of an older time. He freely offers Orlando "five hundred crowns" (38), which represents "the thrifty hire I saved under your father" (39). He boasts of his virility: "Though I look old, yet I am strong and lusty" (47). He attributes his heartiness to clean living:

For in my youth I never did apply
Hot and rebellious liquors in my blood,
Nor did with unbashful forehead woo
The means of weakness and debility. (48–51)

He is an ideal type of the old man, whose age has not, like Macbeth's, "fall'n into the sear, the yellow leaf" (5.3.23). Old Adam's age "is as a lusty winter, / Frosty, but kindly" (52–53). Interestingly, Shakespeare is reputed to have played Old Adam.

The old shepherd Corin is an analogous figure to Duke Senior and Old Adam. He plays the role of a simple and virtuous old man, a type right out of the conventions of pastoral and its assumptions about the simple life lived close to nature. In his wit combat with the courtly and sophisticated Touchstone, he gives as good as he gets from the clown's satirical wit. He is clearly joking when he answers Touchstone's question: "Hast any philosophy in thee, shepherd?" (3.2.21–22) by presenting him with a series of meaningless equivalences:

> I know the more one sickens, the worse at ease he is; and that he that wants money, means, and content is without three good friends; that the property of rain is to wet and fire to burn; that good pasture makes fat sheep, and that a great cause of the night is lack of the sun. (23–28)

This is like Antony's spoofing of Lepidus in *Antony and Cleopatra*, where he states that the crocodile "is shaped, sir, like itself, and it is as broad as it hath breadth; it is just so high as it is, and moves with it own organs" (2.7.43–45). Corin expresses a pastoral ideal similar to Duke Senior's: "I earn that I eat, get that I wear, owe no man hate, envy no man's happiness, glad of other men's good, content with my harm; and the greatest of my pride is to see my ewes graze and my lambs suck" (3.2.73–77). This is like the naturalism of Poor Tom in *King Lear* as "unaccommodated man" (3.4.105).

Gonzalo in *The Tempest* is an old lord who exudes a sweet reasonableness. In the cast of characters he is listed as "an honest old councilor." We see him first during the tempest at the beginning of the play. Despite the storm, he manages to maintain his patience and good humor. At the very end of the scene, when the ship has split in half and everyone is drowning, he wittily remarks: "Now would I give a thousand furlongs of sea for an acre of barren ground—long heath, brown furze, anything. The wills above be done, but I would fain die a dry death" (1.1.64–67). He is a true believer in providence.

In Prospero's long expository speech to Miranda in the next scene, we again see Gonzalo in a positive and beneficial light. In the "rotten carcass of a butt" (1.2.146) given to Prospero and his daughter in their exile from Milan, Gonzalo "out of his charity" (162) provides them with food, fresh water, and "rich garments, linens, stuffs, and necessaries" (164). To advance Prospero's "art," or magic, Gonzalo "of his gentleness" (165) supplies the magician with the necessary tools of his craft:

> Knowing I loved my books, he furnished me
> From mine own library with volumes that
> I prize above my dukedom. (166–68)

Prospero's brother, Antonio, who has usurped his kingdom, and Sebastian, his co-conspirator and brother of the king of Naples, make fun of Gonzalo, whom they call "old cock" (32) and "this ancient morsel, this Sir Prudence" (2.1.290). By his own admission he is an old man whose "old bones ache" (3.3.2), but his presentation of his ideal commonwealth is full of imagination and exuberance. It owes an obvious debt to Montaigne, but it is also related to other contemporary utopias, being full of heterodox, anarchistic, and libertarian ideas:

> I' th' commonwealth I would by contraries
> Execute all things. For no kind of traffic [trade]
> Would I admit; no name of magistrate. (2.1.152–54)

Gonzalo says that "letters," or learning, should not be known and presumably that riches and poverty would then disappear. His most unusual stipulation is that there be

> No occupation; all men idle, all;
> And women too, but innocent and pure;
> No sovereignty. (159–61)

It is truly an idealistic, socialist vision: "All things in common nature should produce" (164). In sum: "I would with such perfection govern, sir, / T' excel the Golden Age" (172–73). Gonzalo's ideal commonwealth reproduces the Golden Age feeling of Duke Senior's pastoral kingdom in *As You Like It*.

At the end of the play all members of the shipwrecked wedding party are Prospero's prisoners, including, as Ariel reports,

> Him that you termed, sir, the good old Lord Gonzalo.
> His tears runs down his beard like winter's drops
> From eaves of reeds [as on a thatched roof]. (5.1.15–17)

Prospero expostulates to everyone in his charmed circle, but only Gonzalo is exempt from recrimination:

> Holy Gonzalo, honorable man,
> Mine eyes, ev'n sociable to the show of thine,
> Fall fellowly drops. (62–64)

Prospero is deeply moved and remembers Gonzalo's kindness to him:

> O good Gonzalo,
> My true preserver, and a loyal sir
> To him thou follow'st, I will pay thy graces
> Home both in word and deed. (68–71)

Presumably Gonzalo accompanies Prospero back to Milan and resumes his high office in the state. Gonzalo is very different from Prospero. Both are old men, but Gonzalo is the good and wise old man, whereas Prospero is cunning, artful, and manipulative.

Some characters in Shakespeare are not wise old men at the beginning of the play—like Duke Senior, Old Adam, and Gonzalo—but are endowed with a special wisdom shortly before their deaths. One thinks of Henry IV in *2 Henry IV* and Richard II. Henry is grievously sick in act 4, scene 4, and the next scene is his last. He is dead by act 5, when his son, Harry, is invested as King Henry V. Shortly before his death, however, Henry has an illuminating scene of reflection and quiet meditation. It begins with the king entering *"in his nightgown"* (3.1), or dressing gown, followed by a long soliloquy that is an apostrophe to sleep. As he explains to his son in a later scene, the king is suffering from a guilty conscience:

> God knows, my son,
> By what bypaths and indirect crooked ways
> I met this crown, and I myself know well
> How troublesome it sat upon my head. (4.5.183–86)

As a result the king cannot sleep:

> O sleep, O gentle sleep,
> Nature's soft nurse, how have I frighted thee,
> That thou no more wilt weigh my eyelids down
> And steep my senses in forgetfulness? (3.1.5–8)

Sleep comes to all sorts of persons—even in perilous situations like the ship-boy "upon the high and giddy mast" (18)—but not to the king. The conclusion is obvious: "Then happy low [lowborn], lie down! / Uneasy lies the head that wears a crown" (30–31).

The king is in an unusually meditative mood, reflecting the fact that he is near the end of his life. He at first considers the body of his kingdom—"How foul it is, what rank diseases grow" (39)—but then proceeds to a larger topic: "O God, that one might read the book of fate, / And see the revolution of the times" (45–46). His attempt to grasp the nature of history and his speculations are like Macbeth's insistent questions to the Witches:

> though the treasure
> Of nature's germens tumble all together,
> Even till destruction sicken, answer me
> To what I ask you. (4.1.58–61)

This speech also recalls Lear caught in the storm and asking "all-shaking thunder" to "crack nature's moulds, all germens spill at once / That make ingrateful man!" (3.2.8–9). Germens are the seeds of all life. Thus, Henry is trying to establish some meaningful causation in the "revolution of the times."

But the role of chance is powerful, and the king is filled with melancholy thoughts:

> How chances, mocks,
> And changes fill the cup of alteration
> With divers liquors! (3.1.51–53)

Fortunately one cannot predict the future, for if this were so "the happiest youth . . . would shut the book, and sit him down and die" (54–56). Next, the king thinks of examples from his own reign, especially Northumberland,

> the man nearest my soul,
> Who like a brother toiled in my affairs
> And laid his love and life under my foot. (61–63)

Yet Northumberland eventually proves a traitor, as Richard II—the man whom Henry (then simply Bolingbroke) deposed and had murdered—remembers so unforgettably in prophetic terms: "Northumberland, thou ladder by the which / My cousin Bolingbroke ascends my throne" (70–71). The king is trying to understand the revolution of the times that has brought him to the throne and now presages his imminent death.

Warwick, an important counselor to the king, completes his thoughts, bringing his speculations to a philosophical conclusion:

> There is a history in all men's lives,
> Figuring the nature of the times deceased,
> The which observed, a man may prophesy,
> With a near aim, of the main chance of things

As yet not come to life, who in their seeds
And weak beginning lie intreasurèd.
Such things become the hatch and brood of time. (80–86)

It is interesting that Warwick uses the seed image, which continues
the idea of "germens," and that this provides an explanation for the
revolution of the times. The "hatch and brood of time" contains within
it the shape of things to come. So a philosophical man may prophesy
"the main chance of things / As yet not come to life." In other words,
there is a preordained order of events. Despite appearances, things do
not happen by mere chance, as evidenced by the image of the ladder in
Richard II's prophecy about Northumberland. Henry IV, now sick and
near death, at least is reassured that what has happened during his
reign are not mere random, chance occurrences but "necessities" (92).
He is ready to "meet them like necessities" (93).

Richard II undergoes a strong transformation during the course of
the play of the same name. After he has been deposed by Bolingbroke
(who becomes King Henry IV), imprisoned, and is about to be murdered, he comes to a new philosophical awareness of his condition and
the reality that surrounds him. While incarcerated in Pomfret Castle,
he delivers a long, meditative soliloquy:

I have been studying how I may compare
This prison where I live unto the world:
And for because the world is populous,
And here is not a creature but myself,
I cannot do it. Yet I'll hammer it out. (5.5.1–5)

By examining his thoughts Richard tries to emerge from his microcosm,
or "little world" (9), and to understand his present situation, which will
surely end in his imminent death. He sees himself, somewhat histrioni-
cally, as an actor playing many roles:

Thus play I in one person many people,
And none contented; sometimes am I a king,

Then treasons make me wish myself a beggar,
And so I am. Then crushing penury
Persuades me I was better when a king. (31–35)

He is acutely conscious of being "nothing" (38), like his earlier, mournful thoughts when he was deposed:

I have no name, no title,
No, not that name was given me at the font
But 'tis usurped. (4.1.254–56)

He has become "a mockery king of snow" (259). In his prison cell he is preoccupied with his present pitiful and pitiable status:

But whate'er I be,
Nor I, nor any man that but man is,
With nothing shall be pleased, till he be eased
With being nothing. (5.5.38–41)

He is preparing himself spiritually for death.

In his soliloquy Richard takes up images from the reality that surrounds him and analogizes them. He hears music that is out of tune and thinks immediately of "the music of men's lives" (44). In his own life he "had not an ear to hear my true time broke. / I wasted time, and now doth Time waste me" (48–49). Richard next pursues images of time, specifically clock time: "For now hath Time made me his numb'ring clock" (50). The sounds that tell the hour "are clamorous groans which strike upon my heart, / Which is the bell" (56–57). In his grieving Richard has become philosophical. When a groom of his stable appears to comfort him, Richard moralizes on his horse, Barbary, now ridden by Bolingbroke. His dear horse has no sense of loyalty to his former master, but Richard checks himself:

Forgiveness, horse! Why do I rail on thee,
Since thou created to be awed by man

Wast born to bear? I was not made a horse,
And yet I bear a burden like an ass,
Spurred, galled, and tired by jauncing Bolingbroke. (90–94)

At this late point in the play, when he is about to die, we sense that Richard has not only grown much older than he seemed earlier but also much wiser. He is suddenly aware of his spiritual condition, and he speaks philosophically, like Hamlet in his soliloquies.

Lastly, I wish to consider the wisdom of Portia's dead father in *The Merchant of Venice*, who has prescribed that his daughter marry the suitor who rightly chooses the casket containing her likeness. Portia is annoyed that she cannot choose a husband for herself: "I may neither choose who I would nor refuse who I dislike, so is the will of a living daughter curbed by the will of a dead father" (1.2.22–25). Nevertheless she is determined to follow the dictates of her dead father: "If I live to be as old as Sibylla [the Cumean Sibyl], I will die as chaste as Diana unless I be obtained by the manner of my father's will"(105–7). The episode of the three caskets has a folkloric quality suggesting that everything will work out well in the end. Nerissa, her waiting gentlewoman, is certain of the rightness of Portia's father's "imposition" (104–5). Portia believes that "the lott'ry of my destiny / Bars me the right of voluntary choosing" (2.1.15–16). There is something magical, of course, in the fact that no suitor has thus far chosen the right casket. The Prince of Morocco opts for the gold and the Prince of Aragon for the silver, leaving only one unselected casket. We therefore feel confident that Bassanio is certain to choose correctly. Nevertheless, the suspense is maintained, even as Portia asserts the wisdom of her dead father's "wit" (18), or intellect, to reassure Bassanio: "If you do love me, you will find me out" (3.2.41).

7. FALSTAFF

Falstaff appears in *1* and *2 Henry IV* and *The Merry Wives of Windsor,* with his death reported in *Henry V.* He is a type of the fat and pleasure-loving young old man who nevertheless remains youthful in spirit.[1] Although he is always spoken of as old, in the scene in *1 Henry IV* where he impersonates the king and Prince Hal plays him, he says: "As I think, his age some fifty, or, by'r Lady, inclining to threescore" (2.4.423–24). Thus Falstaff must be in his mid-to-late fifties. Of course, he is likely to be shaving a few years off his age in order to create the illusion of youth. Remember that Shakespeare died when he was fifty-two. In this same scene Prince Hal, speaking as his father the king, reviles Falstaff: "There is a devil haunts thee in the likeness of an old fat man; a tun of man is thy companion" (446–48). He subsequently describes him as "that villainous abominable misleader of youth, / Falstaff, that old white-bearded Satan" (461–62). Falstaff speaks feelingly in his own defense: "That he is old, the more the pity, his white hairs do witness it" (467–68). He argues: "If to be old and merry be a sin, then many an old host that

I know is damned" (472–73). Hal's final cryptic answer is full of foreboding: "I do, I will" (481). This definitely presages the rejection of Falstaff in *2 Henry IV* when Prince Hal becomes king.

Falstaff's role as the young old man is stressed in the scene with the Lord Chief Justice in *2 Henry IV*. He is the last person Falstaff wants to meet. Now that Prince Hal is king, everything seems to have changed. Falstaff immediately establishes the fact that the Lord Chief Justice is old: "Your lordship, though not clean past your youth, hath yet some smack of an age in you, some relish of the saltness of time in you" (1.2.99–102). He wants to prevent the Lord Chief Justice from what he knows he is about to say, namely, that Falstaff has "misled the youthful Prince" (149), who has now become king. Falstaff tries to parry the Lord Chief Justice's accusations with wit. When the latter remarks that Falstaff's "means are very slender and your waste is great" (145–46), he answers with a pun: "I would it were otherwise. I would my means were greater and my waist slender" (147–48). To the Lord Chief Justice's comment that "there is not a white hair in your face but should have his effect of gravity" (166–67), Falstaff replies: "His effect of gravy, gravy, gravy" (168).

This scene is intentionally detailed and explicit in order to drive home the point about youth and age. Falstaff cleverly reverses the terms of the argument. He addresses the Lord Chief Justice as an old man:

> You that are old consider not the capacities of us that are young.
> You do measure the heat of our livers with the bitterness of your
> galls. And we that are in the vaward [vanguard] of our youth, I
> must confess, are wags too. (180–84)

The Lord Chief Justice is becoming more perturbed by the unorthodox nature of the conversation, and he vents his anger by attributing to Falstaff all the conventional attributes of old age:

> Do you set down your name in the scroll of youth, that are
> written down old with all the characters of age? Have you not a

moist eye, a dry hand, a yellow cheek, a white beard, a decreas-
ing leg, an increasing belly? Is not your voice broken, your
wind short, your chin double, your wit single [feeble], and
every part about you blasted with antiquity, and will you yet
call yourself young? (185–92)

This catalogue of the physical infirmities of old age is more appropriate
to Jaques's "Seven Ages of Man" speech in *As You Like It* (2.7.139–66) than
to the Falstaff we see on the stage.

Unperturbed by the Lord Chief Justice's utterly conventional cata-
loguing of the various ills of old age, Falstaff responds with vigor and
imagination, all the while lying with great conviction:

My lord, I was born about three of the clock in the afternoon,
with a white head and something a round belly. For my voice,
I have lost it with hallowing and singing of anthems. To approve
my youth further, I will not. The truth is, I am only old in
judgment and understanding. (194–99)

Falstaff also celebrates his military prowess. He is not bashful about
exploiting to the full his role of *miles gloriosus*, the glorified but completely cowardly soldier from the play by Plautus. He reminds the Lord
Chief Justice of his important status on the battlefield: "If ye will needs
say I am an old man, you should give me rest. I would to God my name
were not so terrible to the enemy as it is" (225–28). Falstaff ends the
scene with a reference to his gout: " 'Tis no matter if I do halt [limp]—I
have the wars for my color [excuse]" (256–57). The gout may be caused by
the pox—"A pox of this gout! Or a gout of this pox!" (254)—but it doesn't
matter since "a good wit will make use of anything. I will turn diseases
to commodity [advantage]" (258–59).

Falstaff's wit is strongly linked to his youthfulness. No one can put
him down; he is infinitely resourceful verbally. This is the essence of
the *miles gloriosus* role: the pretend soldier must be able to speak heroically. Falstaff has no interest in abstractions such as courage, bravery,
and honor. Recall Hotspur's heroic exclamation in *1 Henry IV*:

By heaven, methinks it were an easy leap
To pluck bright honor from the pale-faced moon,
Or dive into the bottom of the deep,
Where fathom line could never touch the ground,
And pluck up drownèd honor by the locks. (1.3.199–203)

Hotspur is intimately associated with honor, as Prince Hal is not—and
perhaps there lies the seed of Hotspur's doom.

Falstaff will have nothing to do with honor. In a soliloquy toward
the end of the play he asks some telling questions about honor as a personified abstraction:

Can honor set to a leg? No. Or an arm? No. Or take away the
grief of a wound? No. Honor hath no skill in surgery then? No.
What is honor? A word. What is in that word honor? What is
that honor? Air—a trim [nice] reckoning! Who hath it? He that
died a Wednesday. (5.1.131–36)

That is why Falstaff likes "not such grinning honor as Sir Walter hath"
(5.3.58–59)—Sir Walter Blunt, who has just been killed in battle. Falstaff's
ethos is: "Give me life; which if I can save, so; if not, honor comes un-
looked for, and there's an end" (59–61). After Prince Hal has killed
Hotspur, he sees Falstaff lying on the ground and eulogizes him. Yet
the stage direction states that Falstaff *"riseth up"* (5.4.109). He is not coun-
terfeiting death: "To die is to be a counterfeit" (114–15). Falstaff's guid-
ing principle remains: "The better part of valor is discretion, in the
which better part I have saved my life" (119–20).

The central idea is that Falstaff is a consummate actor, and that he is
brilliant in the role of the young old man. In the scene, mentioned earlier, where he plays Prince Hal's father, King Henry IV, and the Prince
plays him, he carefully prepares for the role. Before he is ready to begin,
he sets up the properties and the scene: "This chair shall be my state
[throne], this dagger my scepter, and this cushion my crown" (2.4.378–79).
He instructs Hal: "Give me a cup of sack to make my eyes look red, that
it may be thought I have wept; for I must speak in passion, and I will do

it in King Cambyses' vein" (384–87). King Cambyses was a ranting tyrant in a play by Thomas Preston entitled *A Lamentable Tragedie, mixed full of plesant mirth* (1569). We can gather how successful the acting is from the approving comments of the audience—in the person of Mistress Quickly, the hostess of the Eastcheap tavern. Falstaff acts like a consummate professional, just as Hamlet, following the success of the "Mousetrap" play, says to Horatio: "Would not this, sir, and a forest of feathers—if the rest of my fortunes turn Turk with me—with two Provincial roses on my razed shoes, get me a fellowship in a cry of players?" (3.2.281–84). Falstaff and Hamlet both pride themselves on their histrionic ability.

Falstaff in love in *2 Henry IV* represents the pinnacle of his acting ability—at least according to Poins, Prince Hal's companion: "Is it not strange that desire should so many years outlive performance?" (2.4.267–68). This same scene discloses Falstaff's amorous relation to Doll Tearsheet, an available woman in Mistress Quickly's tavern. There are many references here to Falstaff's advancing years; indeed he seems older and less vigorous in the second part of *Henry IV* than in the first. At the very beginning of the scene Francis and another drawer, or tapster, discuss "apple-johns," a kind of apple that ripened around St. John's Day (June 24) but was only eaten (after two years) when it shriveled up and withered. Francis announces that Falstaff "cannot endure an apple-john" (2–3), and the nameless drawer recounts that Prince Hal "once set a dish of apple-johns before him, and told him there were five more Sir Johns, and, putting off his hat, said, 'I will now take my leave of these six dry, round, old, withered knights.' It ang'red him to the heart" (4–9)—presumably because the apple-john signifies an impotent old man.

After Doll has unceremoniously discharged Pistol from her company for swaggering, she turns affectionately to Falstaff:

Ah, you sweet little rogue, you! Alas, poor ape, how thou sweat'st! Come, let me wipe thy face. Come on, you whoreson chops [fat cheeks]. Ah, rogue! I' faith, I love thee. Thou art as valorous as Hector of Troy, worth five of Agamemnon, and ten times better than the Nine Worthies. Ah, villain! (220–25)

One is reminded of Gertrude's affectionate words to her son during the fatal fencing match in *Hamlet*: "He's fat [sweaty], and scant of breath. / Here, Hamlet, take my napkin, rub thy brows" (5.2.288–89), and again after she has drunk the contents of the poisoned cup: "Come, let me wipe thy face" (295). Doll's words recall the leading characters of *Troilus and Cressida* and the Nine Worthies play-within-a-play of *Love's Labor's Lost*, endowing Falstaff with heroic stature.

There is a mixture in this scene of lively sensual attraction and *memento mori* (remembrances of death). Doll speaks familiarly to Falstaff: "Thou whoreson little tidy Bartholomew boar-pig, when wilt thou leave fighting o' days and foining [thrusting] o' nights, and begin to patch up thine old body for heaven?" (2.4.235–38). This kind of talk is disturbing to Falstaff: "Peace, good Doll! Do not speak like a death's-head. Do not bid me remember mine end" (239–40). Falstaff is acutely aware of his failing age, repeating: "I am old, I am old" (278), to which Doll replies: "I love thee better than I love e'er a scurvy young boy of them all" (279–80). Prince Hal and Poins provide a satirical commentary on the amorous scene. Prince Hal jokes: "Look whe'r [whether] the withered elder hath not his poll [hair] clawed like a parrot" (265–66) and "Saturn and Venus this year in conjunction! What says th' almanac to that?" (270–71). Saturn, the father of Zeus, was associated with old age, the opposite of Venus. Their astrological conjunction, or connection of qualities, was regarded as rare or impossible. This scene ends on a sentimental note, with Doll exiting "blubbered" (in tears) and confessing: "If my heart be not ready to burst—well, sweet Jack, have a care of thyself" (388–89). Mistress Quickly also praises Falstaff: "I have known thee these twenty-nine years, come peascod time, but an honester and truer-hearted man—well, fare thee well" (391–93).

This explains why the rejection of Falstaff in act 5, scene 5, is such an emotional event. There are abundant reasons—chief among them the character of Prince Hal—to anticipate it right from the beginning of *1 Henry IV*, but it is still a wrenching and seemingly tragic event. King Henry V, formerly Prince Hal, speaks sternly and moralistically:

I know thee not, old man. Fall to thy prayers.
How ill white hairs becomes a fool and jester!
I have long dreamt of such a kind of man,
So surfeit-swelled, so old, and so profane. (48–51)

The emphasis is on "old man," mention of which confirms Falstaff's worst fears. The king's speech obliterates the myth of the young old man that Falstaff has tried so hard to perpetuate.

Falstaff never recovers from his rejection at the end of *2 Henry IV*. His death is reported in a very moving scene in *Henry V*. It is interesting that in this same play the Welsh captain Fluellen recounts the rejection of Falstaff as if it were a momentous historical event. In the manner of Plutarch's parallel lives of the noble Greeks and Romans, the learned Fluellen draws a parallel between the life of King Henry V and that of Alexander the Great:

Alexander, God knows, and you know, in his rages, and his
furies, and his wraths, and his cholers, and his moods, and
his displeasures, and his indignations, and also being a little
intoxicates in his prains, did, in his ales and his angers, look you,
kill his best friend, Cleitus. (4.7.35–41)

Fluellen draws the parallel at length:

As Alexander killed his friend Cleitus, being in his ales and his
cups, so also Harry Monmouth, being in his right wits and his
good judgments, turned away the fat knight with the great-belly
doublet—he was full of jests, and gipes, and knaveries, and
mocks; I have forgot his name. (47–52)

The English captain Gower reminds him that his name is Sir John Falstaff. This is a fitting memorial to Falstaff since Alexander needed to be drunk in order to kill his close friend Cleitus in 328 B.C. So Fluellen imagines it some great aberration of King Henry V to turn away "the fat knight with the great-belly doublet." Of course, this is not what actually happens. Hal is sober and knows exactly what he is doing.

Falstaff reappears in a very different guise in *The Merry Wives of Windsor*. There is a tradition that the play was written at the request of Queen Elizabeth, who "commanded it to be finished in fourteen days." This is based upon John Dennis's dedication of *The Comical Gallant* (1702) to George Granville. In his 1709 edition of Shakespeare's works, Nicolas Rowe expands on these comments. According to the latter, the queen "was so well pleas'd with that admirable Character of *Falstaff*, in the two Parts of *Henry* the Fourth, that she commanded him to continue it for one Play more, and to shew him in Love."[2]

The Merry Wives of Windsor represents Shakespeare's only attempt to write a city comedy rivaling the many contemporary comedies about London life. However, Shakespeare's play is not set in London but in the town of Windsor. In the play Shakespeare makes a conscious attempt to imitate the colloquial speech of tradesmen. This play presents quite a different Falstaff from the one that appears in the *Henry IV* plays. In an effort to repair his fortunes and improve his luck, he makes love simultaneously to two tradesmen's wives, Mistress Ford and Mistress Page. Both of the women are impervious to Falstaff's advances and express their moral indignation at his impudence. The play is filled with colorful folkloric tidbits about Windsor. The myth of Falstaff as the youthful old man is exploded immediately by Mistress Page upon receiving his love letter: "O wicked, wicked world. One that is well-nigh worn to pieces with age to show himself a young gallant!" (2.1.20–22). Mistress Ford is equally indignant: "What tempest, I trow, threw this whale, with so many tuns of oil in his belly, ashore at Windsor? How shall I be revenged on him? I think the best way were to entertain him with hope till the wicked fire of lust have melted him in his own grease" (62–67). This is not the old, witty Falstaff of the *Henry IV* plays. The revenges of the merry wives are both farcical and moralistic.

Justice Shallow in *2 Henry IV* and *The Merry Wives of Windsor* is a countertype—almost a parody of—Falstaff. There are two references to his age. When Shallow is reminiscing in *2 Henry IV* about Jane Nightwork, a "bona-roba" (209), or prostitute, Falstaff tells him that she is "old, old, Master Shallow" (3.2.211). Shallow agrees: "Nay, she must be old. She cannot choose but be old. Certain she's old, and had Robin Nightwork by old Nightwork before I came to Clement's Inn [a law school]" (212–15). Silence, Shallow's fellow justice, specifies the time: "That's fifty-five year ago" (216). It's unusual for Shakespeare to mention a specific time, but that would put Shallow in his mid-seventies or older. In *The Merry Wives of Windsor* Shallow says that he has "lived fourscore years and upward" (3.1.53). That would make him exactly the age of King Lear, which seems improbable, but since Shallow and Falstaff were contemporaries at Clement's Inn, Shallow's age bears on how old we assume Falstaff is.

Shallow's main appearance occurs in act 3, scene 2, of *2 Henry IV*. A justice of the peace residing in the country, his reminiscences concerning his reckless youth make him a rather ridiculous figure. He is constantly boasting of "the mad days that I have spent!" (34–35) while at the same time lamenting "how many of my old acquaintance are dead!" (35–36). Like Sir Andrew Aguecheek in *Twelfth Night*, he naively admires what he considers to be sophisticated speech. When Bardolph, Falstaff's red-nosed companion, remarks that "a soldier is better accommodated than with a wife" (69–70), Shallow is surprisingly taken with Bardolph's diction—although no one else ever is: "It is well said, in faith, sir, and it is well said indeed too. 'Better accommodated'! It is good, yea, indeed, is it. Good phrases are surely, and ever were, very commendable. 'Accommodated'! It comes of *'accommodo.'* Very good, a good phrase" (71–75). Shallow is a tedious and repetitive old man, like Polonius in *Hamlet*, but he is probably more like the pedantic schoolmaster Holofernes in *Love's Labor's Lost*. Falstaff never picks up stylistic bits from the conversation of others: he is not only witty in himself "but the cause that wit is in other men" (*2 Henry IV,* 1.2.10–11).

Shallow is delighted with Falstaff, whereas the latter more or less tolerates the former, who luxuriates in amorous recollections of his madcap youth: "O, Sir John, do you remember since we lay all night in the Windmill [a brothel?] in Saint George's Field?" (3.2.199–200). Falstaff is not eager to continue the conversation: "No more of that, Master Shallow" (201), but Shallow is unstoppable: "Ha! 'Twas a merry night.

And is Jane Nightwork alive?" (202–3). Shallow enlists the elderly Silence as a fellow celebrant: "Ha, cousin Silence, that thou hadst seen that that this knight and I have seen! Ha, Sir John, said I well?" (217–18). Falstaff only reluctantly adds: "We have heard the chimes at midnight" (220). Yet he can't rein in Shallow's repetitious exuberance: "That we have, that we have, that we have, in faith, Sir John, we have" (222–23). Falstaff mocks Shallow's maudlin feeling of nostalgia for the past, a characteristic of old men with which Falstaff does not wish to be associated.

At the end of this scene, Falstaff has a long soliloquy in which he enlightens us about the Justice: "Lord, Lord, how subject we old men are to this vice of lying! This same starved justice hath done nothing but prate to me of the wildness of his youth, and the feats he hath done about Turnbull Street [a disreputable area], and every third word a lie" (312–16). The point is that Falstaff, a true wit, wishes to distance himself from Shallow, who is foolish and witless. He remembers Shallow at Clement's Inn, "like a man made after supper of a cheese-paring. When 'a was naked, he was, for all the world, like a forked radish, with a head fantastically carved upon it with a knife . . . yet lecherous as a monkey, and the whores called him mandrake [a forked root in the shape of a man's genitals]" (318–21, 323–25). Falstaff intends to make use of Shallow's wealth when he returns. As he puts it in an off-color pun: "And't shall go hard but I'll make him a philosopher's two stones to me" (339–40). In alchemy the philosopher's stone was supposed to turn base metal into gold, whereas the philosopher's two stones are his testicles.

Toward the end of 2 Henry IV, while Falstaff is awaiting his triumphant reception by Prince Hal (who has become King Henry V), there is a celebratory drinking scene with Shallow and Silence. Silence is drunk and sings a merry catch, to the surprise of Falstaff: "I did not think Master Silence had been a man of this mettle" (5.3.38–39). Then Silence speaks one of the most memorable—and pitiable—lines ever spoken by an old man in all of Shakespeare: "Who, I? I have been merry twice and once ere now" (40–41). This is truly elegiac. Later in the scene Silence kneels and sings:

Do me right,
And dub me knight.
Samingo. (74–76)

Samingo refers to a Monsieur Mingo from a popular drinking song, but the name is derived from the Latin *mingere,* to make water. Silence asks for Falstaff's agreement: "Is't not so?" Falstaff replies " 'Tis so," and Silence concludes: "Is't so? Why then, say an old man can do somewhat" (77–80). Not much but somewhat. This is Silence's unforgettable contribution to the old man theme of *2 Henry IV.*

8. JEALOUS OLD MEN:

OTHELLO AND LEONTES

The Winter's Tale is modeled on *Othello*. Both Leontes and Othello[1] imagine themselves the victims of adulteries and see themselves as cuckolds. Unlike *Othello*, however, *The Winter's Tale* is a tragicomedy and ends happily. In both plays jealousy appears as a kind of madness, which is more believable psychologically in *Othello* because it is developed gradually from Iago's clever insinuations. In *The Winter's Tale* jealousy descends upon Leontes with a sudden and inexplicable fury. In folklore a cuckold is usually a comic figure. He is generally depicted as an old man—the *pantalone* of the commedia dell'arte—who has married a young and beautiful wife whom one feels he is incapable of satisfying sexually. Shakespeare is thus working against the grain in both *Othello* and *The Winter's Tale*—at least in the first half of the latter play—in making the protagonists tragic.

The word "cuckold" occurs four times in *Othello*. Iago first uses it in a sportive way to set on his gull Roderigo: "If thou canst cuckold him [Othello], thou dost thyself a pleasure, me a sport" (1.3.364–65). Sex is a game for Iago, not something that involves strong feelings. In the temptation scene Iago delights in tormenting Othello:

> That cuckold lives in bliss
> Who, certain of his fate, loves not his wronger;
> But O, what damned minutes tells he o'er
> Who dotes, yet doubts—suspects, yet fondly loves! (3.3.167–70)

We can see what stylistic pleasure Iago takes in his little flourishes—the half-rhyme of "dotes, yet doubts."

Othello uses "cuckold" only once: "I will chop her [Desdemona] into messes! Cuckold me!" (4.1.202). It is definitely a frightening word for him. Finally, in her bantering conversation with Desdemona, Emilia, like her husband, makes light of the idea of cuckoldry: "Why, who would not make her husband a cuckold to make him a monarch? I should venture purgatory for't" (4.3.77–79). However, the innocent Desdemona cannot imagine doing such a wrong "for the whole world" (81). The relation between Desdemona and Emilia, and the fact that they are worlds apart in terms of discourse, is strikingly like that between Juliet and the Nurse in *Romeo and Juliet*.

Almost from the beginning of the play Othello is identified as old. In the chaotic first scene Iago takes the lead in shouting up to Brabantio, who is located on the upper stage, that his daughter has eloped with Othello: "Even now, now, very now, an old black ram / Is tupping your white ewe. Arise, arise!" (1.1.85–86). Iago is deliberately salacious and provocative in his frenzied exclamations: "Even now, now, very now." Brabantio is represented as the old father of a beautiful young daughter, like old Capulet and his daughter. Roderigo, a suitor of Desdemona, plays a minor role in this scene. In a later scene Iago is identified as being twenty-eight years old (1.3.306–7), so he is clearly not an "old black ram" like Othello. Later Othello says specifically that he is "declined / Into the vale of years" (3.3.264–65). How old is that? He is definitely not as young as Iago, Cassio, and Roderigo.

Othello is very conscious of his age in relation to the young Desdemona. When she insists with the Venetian senate that she be allowed to accompany him to Cyprus in order that she not be bereft of "the rites for why I love him" (1.3.252), her husband is embarrassed and apologizes to the duke for what has clearly a strongly sexual innuendo:

> Let her have your voice.
> Vouch with me, heaven, I therefore beg it not
> To please the palate of my appetite,
> Nor to comply with heat—the young affects
> In me defunct—and proper satisfaction;
> But to be free and bounteous to her mind. (1.3.255–60)

In other words, he is doing it for her benefit, not his. This is a surprising admission. One finds it hard to grasp why he would want to discredit his sexual powers—"the young affects / In me defunct." Is he, then, like the *pantalone* character of the commedia dell'arte, the proverbial old man who marries a young wife and is thought to be impotent or sexually feeble?

Othello dwells on the fact that he has no intention of putting sexual pleasure before the business of state:

> No, when light-winged toys
> Of feathered Cupid seel with wanton dullness
> My speculative and officed instrument,
> That my disports corrupt and taint my business,
> Let housewives make a skillet of my helm. (1.3.263–67)

These affirmations are a bad beginning for a marriage, and they seem to offer Iago a strong sexual hint of how he should pursue his entrapment of Othello. At the end of this scene he advises Roderigo that Desdemona, like all Venetian women, is easily corruptible: "She must change for youth; when she is sated with his body, she will find the errors of her choice" (1.3.346–48). This is a theme that Iago refuses to abandon, as if he is telling Othello what he already suspects, namely, that this is an unfortunate marriage, almost certain to end in disaster, because of Othello's age and his sexual inadequacy.

Othello dotes on Desdemona, as he confesses when he joins her in Cyprus:

> O my sweet,
> I prattle out of fashion, and I dote
> In mine own comforts. (2.1.203–5)

"Dotes" means to love excessively, beyond the bounds of reason. Bianca "dotes on Cassio, as 'tis the strumpet's plague / To beguile many and be beguiled by one" (4.1.98–99). In the temptation scene Iago teases Othello with the torments of the cuckold: "But O, what damned minutes tells he o'er / Who dotes, yet doubts—suspects, yet fondly loves!" (3.3.169–70). "Dotes" is frequently used by Shakespeare to indicate a love that is beyond all reasonable measure, such as the love Helena feels for Demetrius in *A Midsummer Night's Dream*:

> she, sweet lady, dotes,
> Devoutly dotes, dotes in idolatry,
> Upon this spotted and inconstant man. (1.1.108–10)

Similarly, the love elixir that Oberon places on Titania's eyelids will make her dote "in extremity" (3.2.3) on the first thing she sees—which happens to be Bottom transformed into an ass.

Dotage is particularly connected by Shakespeare with an old man's love—or, if not "old" in our sense of the word, with the desires of a man who feels that his sexual powers are fading. In *Venus and Adonis* the unsatisfied Venus laments: "How love makes young men thrall, and old men dote" (837). This link between dotage and an old man's love fits neatly into Iago's representation of Othello and Desdemona. He expatiates to Roderigo on why it is inevitable that the inflamed love of Othello cannot last: "When the blood is made dull with the act of sport, there should be a game to inflame it and to give satiety a fresh appetite, loveliness in favor, sympathy in years, manners, and beauties; all of which the Moor is defective in" (2.1.225–28). Cassio is young but Othello and Desdemona have no "sympathy in years."

It is strange how effectively Iago's persuasions of Roderigo seem to work retroactively on Othello. In Iago's second act soliloquy—it is surprising how many soliloquies he has—he works out all the erotic implications of Othello's dotage:

> His soul is so enfettered to her love
> That she may make, unmake, do what she list,
> Even as her appetite shall play the god
> With his weak function. (2.3.345–48)

"Weak function" has a definite sexual connotation that recalls what Othello had said earlier about "the young affects / In me defunct" (1.3.258–59).

Another line worth pursuing in terms of Othello's age is his connection with Brabantio, Desdemona's old father. Remember that Othello's wooing speech was originally recited for Brabantio's benefit:

> Her father loved me; oft invited me;
> Still questioned me the story of my life
> From year to year, the battle, sieges, fortune,
> That I have passed.
> I ran it through, even from my boyish days
> To th' very moment that he bade me tell it. (1.3.127–32)

Desdemona listens spellbound to these heroic speeches: "She'd come again, and with a greedy ear / Devour up my discourse" (148–49). Othello then repeats his story in detail—"all my pilgrimage dilate" (152)—and is rewarded with Desdemona's love: "My story being done, / She gave me for my pains a world of kisses" (157–58).

This scene clearly suggests that Othello is Brabantio's friend and, if not an old man like him, at least of comparable years. As an old father solicitous of his young daughter's best interests, Brabantio is like old Egeus, the father of Hermia in *A Midsummer Night's Dream*. Both insist that their daughters were won over by witchcraft. Othello's connection with Brabantio makes his parting words especially dire and prophetic: "Look to her, Moor, if thou hast eyes to see: / She has deceived her father, and may thee" (1.3.287–88).

All these bewildering hints rob Othello of his peace of mind. It is simplistic to believe that the clever and diabolical Iago, the great improviser, seduces the free, open, noble, generous, and innocent Othello. What makes the tragedy especially poignant is that Othello is so vulnerable to the events that befall him that he is, in some very important way, responsible for his own tragedy. After all, he is the one who tells us that he is growing old and that his sexual powers are in decline. When Iago callously reassures Roderigo concerning his suit to woo Desdemona, he seems to be picking up hints from Othello's own misgivings about his capacity as a lover and husband. Iago seems to be teasing him with fears that he himself has about his own sexual powers.

That is what creates the amazing sense of dividedness in Othello, the fact that at the very moment he is most determined to kill Desdemona and take his revenge on her supposed adultery, he is also aware that he may be completely wrong. This proleptic sense of how he will feel at the very end of the play is most evident in his dialogue with Iago in act 4: "Ay, let her rot, and perish, and be damned tonight; for she shall not live. No, my heart is turned to stone; I strike it, and it hurts my hand. O, the world hath not a sweeter creature! She might lie by an emperor's side and command him tasks" (4.1.183–87). In some strange way Othello seems to anticipate his tragic end. That is the meaning of his heart-rending exclamation: "But yet the pity of it, Iago. O Iago, the pity of it, Iago" (197–98). Iago, however, understands nothing of this kind of anguish.

Othello's jealousy provides the pattern for Leontes' jealousy in *The Winter's Tale,* which is much wilder and much less motivated by psychological factors. This is what one would expect in a romance. Aging is important in both plays, but the later play introduces a gap of sixteen years that firmly situates *The Winter's Tale* in a before-and-after pattern. The symbolic figure of Time appears onstage at the beginning of act 4 to explain the abrupt transition. He bears all the traditional attributes found in contemporary emblem books and in the *Sonnets:* he is old, has wings, and carries an hourglass, suggesting to the audience that he has slept during this sixteen-year interval. He does not wield a scythe, as he does in the concluding couplet of Sonnet 123: "This I do vow, and this shall ever be: / I will be true despite thy scythe and thee."

Although Time resembles the choruses in *Henry V* and *2 Henry IV* (specifically Rumor, depicted as full of tongues in the Induction), he is closest in function to Gower in *Pericles,* in which his narrative precedes every act of the play and he also supplies an epilogue. Gower, a fourteenth-century poet, a contemporary of Chaucer, and the author of *Confessio Amantis*, is the main source of *Pericles*. Mostly written in octosyllabic couplets, Gower's diction reflects a medieval-sounding archaism that imitates a sense of the olden times.

Shakespeare's source for *The Winter's Tale* is Robert Greene's *Pandosto: The Triumph of Time* (1588), so it should come as no surprise that Shakespeare introduces the allegorical figure of Time as the chorus to account for the sixteen-year gap at act 4. In attempting to reconcile the audience to this abrupt break in the chronological sequence, Time speaks in his own distinctive style of rhymed, pentameter couplets. Although Shakespeare may be fond of the contrast of before-and-after and the dualistic structure it entails, the sixteen-year gap of *The Winter's Tale* is unusual. The aged figure of Time makes no effort to account for the gap from a rational standpoint. Instead he capriciously remarks:

> I slide
> O'er sixteen years, and leave the growth untried
> Of that wide gap, since it is in my pow'r
> To o'erthrow law, and in one self-born hour
> To plant, and o'erwhelm custom. Let me pass. (4.1.5–9)

Time speaks in the arbitrary and unconfined spirit of romance. He specifies a gap of sixteen years, although in the next scene Camillo, who was Leontes' faithful counselor, says: "It is fifteen years since I saw my country" (4.2.4). Time's speech is a self-conscious interruption of the play's action, as if he alone were in charge of the narrative. Like the chorus in *Henry V,* Time appeals to the audience to use its imaginative powers:

imagine me,
Gentle spectators that I now may be
In fair Bohemia. (4.1.19–21)

However, Time will not reveal the plot and ruin our sense of suspense. He tells us that Perdita is grown up, but

what of her ensues
I list not prophesy; but let Time's news
Be known when 'tis brought forth. (25–27)

Time is not simply an allegorical, emblematic figure. Shakespeare transforms him into a teasing dramatic character like Rumor in *2 Henry IV*.

The editor of the Arden edition of *The Winter's Tale* suggests that Mamillius, Leontes' young son, is about seven years old in act 1, scene 2, which would make Leontes thirty.[2] As he himself says:

Looking on the lines
Of my boy's face, methoughts I did recoil
Twenty-three years, and saw myself unbreeched. (1.2.153–55)

It is unusual for Shakespeare to mention a specific number of years. If one adds the sixteen years that Time accounts for, this would make Leontes at least forty-six in the latter part of the play, although his exact age is not insisted upon. From act 4 to the end of the play Leontes is simply represented as an old man.

Since Leontes and Polixenes, his childhood friend, played together as boys—"We were as twinned lambs, that did frisk i' th' sun" (1.2.67)—they are presumably the same age in act 4. There are a number of references to Polixenes' age in the sheepshearing scene (4.4), especially in relation to his preventing the marriage of his son, Florizel, to the shepherd's daughter (Perdita in disguise). Florizel calls his father "old sir" (360), "ancient sir" (365), and "grave sir" (415). Polixenes swears "by my white beard" (408) against his son's desire to marry without his consent. It is interesting that when Perdita offers flowers to Polixenes and Camillo earlier in the scene, she calls them

> flow'rs
> Of middle summer, and I think they are given
> To men of middle age. (106–8)

She seems to be flattering Polixenes and Camillo. "Middle age" is only used again in Sonnet 7 to refer to the sun in midcourse in the sky. The word clearly does not carry its contemporary connotation since life expectancy was different in Shakespeare's time. Fifty was considered as marking the general onset of old age.

Earlier in her speech Perdita uses the word "ancient" for autumn, which may have some bearing on the phrase "men of middle age":

> the year growing ancient,
> Not yet on summer's death, nor on the birth
> Of trembling winter. (79–81)

Recall that Florizel addresses his father as "ancient sir" (365), which means something like "autumnal," as in Donne's ninth elegy, "The Autumnal": "No *Spring,* nor *Summer* Beauty hath such grace, / As I have seen in one *Autumnal* face."[3] Donne's lines also apply to the statue of Hermione in act 5, scene 3.

The statue scene at the end of the play represents a celebration of married love as the aging Leontes is reunited with his wife, Hermione, thought to be dead during the sixteen-year interval. Under the watchful guidance of Paulina, the wife of Antigonus, another of the king's counselors, Leontes has undergone a long penance for his unjustified jealousy earlier in the play. The first scene of act 5 prepares us for the statue scene, which is relatively brief. Leontes promises never to marry again except by Paulina's "free leave" (70). The latter functions as his spiritual counselor in this scene. Not only that, but she will choose his next wife for him. She warns him that "she shall not be so young / As was your former, but she shall be such / As, walked your first queen's ghost" (78–80). These are clear hints that the real Hermione will return, as is the entrance of Perdita in this scene, which prefigures her mother being brought back to life. The prophecy of the Delphic oracle has been fulfilled: "The King shall live without an heir, if that which is lost be not found" (3.2.132–33).

The wrinkles evident in Hermione's statue are insisted on in order to indicate that she has grown old. Leontes is the first to notice the change:

> But yet, Paulina,
> Hermione was not so much wrinkled, nothing
> So agèd as this seems. (5.3.27–29)

Paulina explains it all as an indication of how artful Julio Romano is:

> So much the more our carver's excellence,
> Which lets go by some sixteen years, and makes her
> As she lived now. (30–32)

Since the strongest criterion of art in Shakespeare is verisimilitude—how closely art imitates life—this is proof of Julio Romano's excellence, namely, that he makes Hermione look sixteen years older than when she was supposed to have died. Recall that Cleopatra, though hardly as old as Hermione, describes herself as "wrinkled deep in time" (*Antony and Cleopatra,* 1.5.29). Old age is consistently described as wrinkled in Shakespeare, as in *Venus and Adonis,* where Venus claims that she is not "hard-favored, foul, or wrinkled old" (133), or in the reference to "wrinkled age" in *The Rape of Lucrece* (275). In *The Taming of the Shrew* Vincentio, the father of Lucentio, is represented as "old, wrinkled, faded, withered" (4.5.43).

In the statue scene Leontes' love for Hermione is developed in terms of warmth. He feels the power of his guilt: "Does not the stone rebuke me, / For being more stone than it?" (37–38). A stone is cold, as is Hermione's statue. One thinks of Othello's anguish, whose "heart is turned to stone; I strike it, and it hurts my hand" (4.1.184–85). According to the medieval and Renaissance physiology of the four humors, old age was characteristically cold and dry. When Paulina commands her to "be stone no more" (99), Hermione suddenly comes alive and steps down from her pedestal. Leontes' first words of wonder are: "Oh, she's warm!" (109), thereby confirming the fact that his old wife is stone no more.

Paulina describes herself at the end of this scene as "an old turtle" (132), or turtledove, who

> Will wing me to some withered bough, and there
> My mate, that's never to be found again,
> Lament till I am lost. (133–35)

Even though *The Winter's Tale* is a romance boasting of many revivifications, Antigonus—and Mamillius—remain securely dead at the end. In the happy ending Paulina is matched with old Camillo. The play ends with Leontes' promise that those involved will be able to expatiate on what has happened, as if they were all characters in a play:

> We may leisurely
> Each one demand and answer to his part
> Performed in this wide gap of time since first
> We were dissevered. (152–55)

The happy ending brings love, warmth, unity, and the promise of a renewed family life. It is the essence of tragicomedy.

9. OLD WARRIORS AND STATESMEN IN THE ENGLISH HISTORY PLAYS

Shakespeare's old warriors in the English history plays are represented as ideal old men: wise in the ways of the world, experienced, loyal, trustworthy, and dedicated to public service.[1] In this chapter I will consider two such characters: Talbot in *1 Henry VI* and Clifford in *2 Henry VI*, both of whom are old soldiers who fight valiantly and heroically for their king.

Talbot is the more fully developed of the two. He is called "old Talbot" when he enters, *"led [by a Servant],"* in act 4, scene 7. He laments the death in battle of his son, John, addressing "thou antic [grotesque] death, which laugh'st us here to scorn" (18), and announcing his own imminent death: "Two Talbots, wingèd through the lither [yielding] sky, / In thy despite shall 'scape mortality" (21–22). Asking for his son's body to be placed in his arms, just before dying he says: "Now my old arms are young John Talbot's grave" (32).

In the very first scene of the play we learn of Talbot's exploits against the French: "Where valiant Talbot, above human thought, / Enacted wonders with his sword and lance" (1.1.121–22). He is not only valiant but also witty and charming, especially with the Countess of Auvergne, who later schemes to trap him. She is astonished by his unimpressive physical stature:

> Is this the scourge of France?
> Is this the Talbot, so much feared abroad
> That with his name the mothers still [silence] their babes?
> I see report is fabulous and false. (2.3.15–18)

Contrary to the laws of hospitality, she practically mocks and scorns him:

> I thought I should have seen some Hercules,
> A second Hector, for his grim aspect
> And large proportion of his strong-knit limbs.
> Alas, this is a child, a silly dwarf!
> It cannot be this weak and writhled [wrinkled] shrimp
> Should strike such terror to his enemies. (19–24)

Talbot assures her that he is but the "shadow" of himself, his "substance" consisting of the troops that surround the countess's castle. He is not offended by her insulting speech. He only desires to "taste of your wine and see what cates [delicate foods] you have" (79). Talbot is both a gentleman and a warrior.

Standing before the town of Bordeaux, Talbot establishes the heroic model that will be closely followed by King Henry V in a later play. If the commanding general of Bordeaux refuses Talbot's offer of peaceful conquest,

> You tempt the fury of my three attendants,
> Lean Famine, quartering Steel, and climbing Fire,
> Who in a moment even [level] with the earth
> Shall lay your stately and air-braving towers. (4.2.9–12)

Even though he is outnumbered, Talbot appeals to the patriotism of his band of brothers: "How are we parked and bounded in a pale, / A little herd of England's timorous deer" (45–46). The scene ends with ringing declarations of heroic defiance:

> Sell every man his life as dear as mine,
> And they shall find dear deer of us, my friends.
> God and Saint George, Talbot and England's right,
> Prosper our colors in his dangerous fight! (53–56)

Talbot endows military conquest with religious and patriotic rhetoric.

Clifford, in 2 Henry VI, is less fully developed than Talbot, but he is also cut from the same heroic cloth. In act 4, scene 8, he enters as "old Clifford" intending to subdue Jack Cade and his rabble in their revolt against the king. He appeals to their patriotism as followers of King Henry VI:

> Is Cade the son of Henry the Fifth,
> That thus you do exclaim you'll go with him?
> Will he conduct you through the heart of France,
> And make the meanest of you earls and dukes? (35–38)

Clifford invokes the glorious vision of Henry V's conquests in France (in a play not yet written) as opposed to the baseness of Cade. Clifford's peroration is like the resounding speeches of Henry V:

> To France, to France! and get what you have lost:
> Spare England, for it is your native coast.
> Henry [King Henry VI] hath money, you are strong and manly;
> God on our side, doubt not of victory. (50–53)

The fact of the matter was that England was already losing much of King Henry V's conquests in France. Clifford is successful in persuading the rabble and Cade sneaks away.

Old statesmen in the English history plays include John of Gaunt in *Richard II* and Cardinal Wolsey in *Henry VIII*. Gaunt is one of seven sons of Edward III, the uncle of Richard II, who is the son of Gaunt's oldest brother, Edward, called the Black Prince. Edmund, Duke of York, is also one of Gaunt's brothers. Thomas of Woodstock, Duke of Gloucester, was another of Gaunt's brothers who was murdered under suspicious circumstances—possibly with the connivance of Richard II. Early in *Richard II* (1.2) the Duchess of Gaunt appeals to Gaunt—in vain—to take revenge for his murdered brother. The very first words of the play, spoken by Richard, identify Gaunt as "Old John of Gaunt, time-honored Lancaster." After his son, Bolingbroke, is exiled, Gaunt complains that he shall not survive the six years of his son's banishment:

My oil-dried lamp and time-bewasted light
Shall be extinct with age and endless night;
My inch of taper will be burnt and done,
And blindfold Death not let me see my son. (1.3.220–23)

These are familiar images of old age and approaching death. The king can do nothing to lengthen Gaunt's life: "Thou canst help time to furrow me with age, / But stop no wrinkle in his pilgrimage" (228–29). It will be recalled that conventional images of time the destroyer are repeated frequently in the *Sonnets*, especially wrinkles.

Act 2, scene 1, begins with the following stage direction: *"Enter John of Gaunt, sick."* (In some productions he is carried onto the stage in a chair.) He speaks prophetically: "Will the King come, that I may breathe my last / In wholesome counsel to his unstaid youth?" (1–2). Gaunt believes that his mortal illness gives him a special authority to impart his wisdom to the wayward king:

O, but they say the tongues of dying men
Enforce attention like deep harmony:
Where words are scarce they are seldom spent in vain,
For they breathe truth that breathe their words in pain. (5–8)

Gaunt draws on moral commonplaces about the portentousness of a dying man's words. It is a well-established formula in praise of old age, of someone near death, to which Gaunt adds additional images:

> The setting sun, and music at the close,
> As the last taste of sweets is sweetest last,
> Writ in remembrance more than things long past. (12–14)

Gaunt hopes that his "death's sad tale may yet undeaf" (16) Richard's ear.

His brother York remains skeptical, but Gaunt is optimistic that his closeness to death will have a strong effect on his nephew Richard:

> Methinks I am a prophet new inspired,
> And thus expiring do foretell of him:
> His rash fierce blaze of riot cannot last,
> For violent fires soon burn out themselves. (31–34)

Next Gaunt launches into an extraordinary—and oft-quoted—invocation of England:

> This blessed plot, this earth, this realm, this England,
> This nurse, this teeming womb of royal kings. (50–51)

But, of course, it is all now corrupted by Richard's misrule:

> This land of such dear souls, this dear dear land—
> Dear for her reputation through the world—
> Is now leased out—I die pronouncing it—
> Like to a tenement [land held by a tenant] or pelting [paltry]
>   farm. (57–60)

This climactic vision of the state of the commonwealth marks the point at which King Richard enters.

Gaunt plays grotesquely on his own name:

O, how that name befits my composition!
Old Gaunt indeed, and gaunt in being old!. . . .
Gaunt am I for the grave, gaunt as a grave
Whose hollow womb inherits naught but bones. (73–74, 82–83)

Richard is already somewhat testy, asking: "Can sick men play so nicely [fastidiously] with their names?" (84). Gaunt, however, cannot be stopped in his bitter condemnation of the king:

Now he that made me knows I see thee ill;
Ill in myself to see, and in thee seeing ill.
Thy deathbed is no lesser than thy land,
Wherein thou liest in reputation sick. (93–96)

Gaunt in his savage rebuke of the King cannot cease punning. He "sees ill," meaning that his eyesight is failing, but "ill" also means evil.

Richard abruptly interrupts Gaunt's catalogue of wrongs: "A lunatic, lean-witted fool, / Presuming on an ague's privilege" (115–16). Richard unceremoniously dismisses Gaunt's contention that "the tongues of dying men / Enforce attention like deep harmony" (5–6). If he were not his uncle, he would have had him beheaded for his offensive speech. Gaunt is totally unsuccessful in making any impression on the king. He even accuses him of murdering his brother Thomas of Woodstock, Duke of Gloucester: "That blood already like the pelican / Hast thou tapped out and drunkenly caroused" (126–27). Gaunt then leaves the stage, presumably to die.

Richard is singularly indifferent to his uncle's death:

The ripest fruit first falls, and so doth he;
His time is spent, our pilgrimage must be;
So much for that. (153–55)

Richard dismissive phrase is curiously echoed by Claudius in *Hamlet* when speaking about young Fortinbras: "So much for him" (1.2.25).

Richard then immediately seizes all of Gaunt's estate (which, according to the laws of inheritance, rightfully belongs to Gaunt's son, Bolingbroke) which the king will use to pay for his Irish wars. This is the final outrage to the memory of Gaunt.

Cardinal Wolsey's downfall and death in *Henry VIII* is also touching, and it contains more of what we have come to expect from tragedy. It is the classic tale of a prince brought low by his own hubris and overweening pride. The conflict is explicitly laid out in the first scene of the play. The Duke of Buckingham, Wolsey's sworn enemy, speaks ill of the cardinal, who has now risen to power under King Henry VIII. His origin is reputed to be that of a butcher's son, and there is great contempt in Buckingham's slangy reference:

> I wonder
> That such a keech can with his very bulk
> Take up [obstruct] the rays o' th' beneficial sun,
> And keep it from the earth. (54–57)

A "keech" is a lump of animal fat. One is reminded of Dame Quickly's reference to "goodwife Keech, the butcher's wife" (*2 Henry IV*, 2.1.94–95). Buckingham also seems to be alluding to Wolsey's obesity. Later in the scene Buckingham develops his slurs: "This butcher's cur is venommouthed, and I / Have not the power to muzzle him" (120–21). Not being noble by birth, Wolsey is ambitious. Norfolk describes him as

> spider-like,
> Out of his self-drawing web, 'a gives us note
> The force of his own merit makes his way. (62–64)

The cardinal combines both malice and potency (105).

Shakespeare goes to great lengths in this scene to develop the character of Wolsey in such a way that readers and audience alike will feel that his downfall is inevitable. He is both proud and revengeful. Buckingham calls him

>   this holy fox,
> Or wolf, or both (for he is equal rav'nous
> As he is subtle, and as prone to mischief
> As able to perform't, his mind and place
> Infecting one another, yea, reciprocally). (158–62)

Buckingham also accuses Wolsey of greed, of buying and selling "his honor as he pleases" (192). It should therefore come as no surprise that Buckingham is arrested for high treason at the end of this scene—presumably at Wolsey's instigation.

Wolsey is subtle, and although he suggests a divorce between Henry and Queen Katherine, his counsels are made in secret. The Lord Chamberlain says:

>   Heaven will one day open
> The King's eyes, that so long have slept upon
> This bold bad man. (2.2.41–43)

In act 2, scene 4, Wolsey pretends to be the queen's compassionate, true friend, but she is wise to him:

> I utterly abhor, yea, from my soul
> Refuse you for my judge, whom, yet once more,
> I hold my most malicious foe, and think not
> At all a friend to truth. (81–84)

She seconds the judgment of Buckingham (1.1) that Wolsey is a dangerous hypocrite:

>   Y'are meek and humble-mouthed.
> You sign your place and calling, in full seeming,
> With meekness and humility, but your heart
> Is crammed with arrogancy, spleen, and pride. (107–10)

The action of the play is moving inevitably toward Wolsey's downfall, which occurs in act 3, scene 2.

Wolsey wants the king to marry the Duchess of Alençon and not Anne Bullen, "a spleeny Lutheran" (3.2.99), whom the king actually marries. That is only one of his numerous blunders. He also accidentally encloses an inventory of his worldly possessions in a packet he sends the king. However, there are even weightier matters. Wolsey realizes that his end is near:

> I shall fall
> Like a bright exhalation in the evening,
> And no man see me more. (225–27)

In his long soliloquy at line 350, he reflects on his tragic fate:

> I have ventured,
> Like little wanton boys that swim on bladders,
> This many summers in a sea of glory,
> But far beyond my depth. My high-blown pride
> At length broke under me and now has left me,
> Weary and old with service, to the mercy
> Of a rude stream that must forever hide me. (358–64)

There is a suggestion throughout that Wolsey's downfall ultimately stems from his humble origins as a butcher's son.

Following his death, an entire scene is devoted to the character of Wolsey. The now sick former Queen Katherine discusses him with Griffith, her Gentleman Usher. The latter speaks only well of him. When Wolsey, a sick man, retires to the abbey at Leicester, Griffith reports him as saying:

> O father abbot,
> An old man broken with the storms of state
> Is come to lay his weary bones among ye;
> Give him a little earth for charity. (4.2.21–24)

There is a newfound humility in Wolsey. As Griffith says, "he died fearing God" (68). It is significant that Shakespeare goes to so much trouble to rehabilitate Wolsey at the end. He is the most interesting character in the play, the only one whose downfall approaches tragedy.

10. FATAL ATTRACTION:

ANTONY AND CLEOPATRA

When Antony returns to Rome early in the play, Cleopatra, awaiting him in Egypt, longs for her absent lover:

> Think on me,
> That am with Phoebus' [the sun god] amorous pinches black
> And wrinkled deep in time. (1.5.27–29)

When Cleopatra undergoes a noble Roman suicide at the end of the play by allowing asps to bite her, she is still thinking in terms of the same imagery: "The stroke of death is as a lover's pinch, / Which hurts and is desired" (5.2.295–96). If Cleopatra is indeed "wrinkled deep in time," how old is she?

As usual, Shakespeare hesitates to give any specific indications of age, except for a messenger's report that Octavia, Antony's new wife, is thirty (3.3.31). John Wilders, the editor of the Arden edition of *Antony and Cleopatra*, says that the historical Cleopatra was born in 69 B.C. and is therefore twenty-nine at the beginning of the play.¹ Clearly Shake-speare imagines her as much older, perhaps in her late thirties and right at the cusp of her child-bearing years. After Cleopatra says that she is "wrinkled deep in time," she reminisces about Caesar and Pompey, her former lovers:

> Broad-fronted Caesar,
> When thou wast here above the ground, I was
> A morsel for a monarch; and great Pompey
> Would stand and make his eyes grow in my brow. (1.5.29–32)

Definitely not a young ingénue like Juliet, she is more like Cressida in *Troilus and Cressida*, a cunning and experienced lover. Perhaps the comparison with Helen in the same play would be even more apt. Cleopatra remembers her "salad days" with Caesar, "when I was green in judgment, cold in blood" (73–74). She was very different then from her present passionate attachment to Antony.

Pompey hopes to keep Antony out of action, relying on Cleopatra to "tie up the libertine in a field of feasts" (2.1.23). He thinks of her as mature and experienced: "Salt Cleopatra, soften thy waned lip!" (21). Admittedly "waned" is the eighteenth-century editor Steevens's emendation for folio "wand," but I think it is one of many references to Cleopatra's waning years. Following Antony's defeat at the battle of Actium, there are many allusions to Cleopatra's age. He inveighs against her with great bitterness: "You were half blasted ere I knew you. Ha!" (3.13.105). "Blasted" is a very strong word, meaning worn out or withered. Recall that in *Richard III* the title character's arm "is like a blasted sapling withered up" (3.4.680), and that the "blasted heath" in *Macbeth* (1.3.77) is the natural setting of the Witches. In particular, "blasted" and related words refer to the destroyed and exploded vigor of natural growth. As the disappointed York complains in *2 Henry VI*: "Thus are my blossoms blasted in the bud, / And caterpillars eat my leaves away" (3.1.89–90). These words are especially important in *Hamlet*. In his angry confrontation with his mother in the closet scene Hamlet contrasts his father's picture with that of Claudius: "Here is your husband, like a mildewed ear / Blasting his wholesome brother" (3.4.65–66). Finally, recall the passionate exclamation by Enobarbus, Antony's chief captain, after Cleopatra's fleet has fled the scene at the battle of Actium: "To see't mine eyes are blasted" (3.10.4).

Antony continues to inveigh against Cleopatra as a "boggler" (3.13.110), or waverer, a woman who seems old from excessive erotic experience:

> I found you as a morsel cold upon
> Dead Caesar's trencher [wooden dish]: nay, you were a fragment
>   [leftover food]
> Of Gneius Pompey's, besides what hotter hours,
> Unregist'red in vulgar fame, you have
> Luxuriously picked out. (116–20)

This food imagery works against any sense of Cleopatra as a fresh, young innocent. In many ways it recalls Ulysses' witty character sketch of Cressida in *Troilus and Cressida*. He refers to her as one of "these encounterers" (4.5.58):

>   set them down
> For sluttish spoils of opportunity
> And daughters of the game. (61–63)

Cleopatra is hardly a "daughter of the game," or prostitute, nor is Cressida, but both are players. Cleopatra's "infinite variety" (2.2.242) excludes her from the world of young lovers.

Antony is consistently represented as aging, while Octavius is spoken of as young. Antony is the last member of the previous Roman generation, as presented in *Julius Caesar,* consisting of heroic figures who have vanished, leaving only the "boy" Octavius. There are many references to Antony's gray hairs. After the battle of Actium, he laments having followed Cleopatra at sea:

> My very hairs do mutiny, for the white
> Reprove the brown for rashness, and they them
> For fear and doting. (3.11.13–15)

He tells Caesar's ambassador: "To the boy Caesar send this grizzled head" (3.13.17). "Grizzled" means gray, or white hairs mixed with brown and black. After Horatio has seen Hamlet's father's ghost, the son questions him: "His beard was grizzled, no?" Horatio replies: "It was as I have seen it in his life, / A sable silvered" (1.2.240–42). After Antony's victory in the second battle with Caesar, he is overjoyed, seeing it as the triumph of age over youth:

> Though gray
> Do something mingle with our younger brown, yet ha' we
> A brain that nourishes our nerves, and can
> Get goal for goal of youth. (4.8.19–22)

There are scattered references throughout the play to Antony as an old man. When he ostentatiously challenges Caesar to single combat, Octavius jokingly replies: "Let the old ruffian know / I have many other ways to die" (4.1.5–7). The word "ruffian" indicates the divide between Antony's old-fashioned manliness and bravado and Caesar's humdrum practicality. In Enobarbus's sardonic aside, this contrast between youth and age is rendered metaphorically: " 'Tis better playing with a lion's whelp / Than with an old one dying" (3.14.94–95). Enobarbus is torn between common sense and loyalty to out-of-date heroic values. His decision to desert Antony leads to his own despair and death.

One of the most powerful aspects of Antony's tragedy is how aware he is of growing old and being in decline. When he calls for servants and no one appears, he remarks: "Authority melts from me" (3.13.90). This is the same problem encountered in *King Lear*, which is also preoccupied with the negative changes that result from old age. Antony's fellow soldier Philo states the problem right at the outset: "Nay, but this dotage of our general's / O'erflows the measure" (1.1.1–2). This is clearly the case because

> His captain's heart,
> Which in the scuffles of great fights hath burst
> The buckles on his breast, reneges all temper

And is become the bellows and the fan
To cool a gypsy's lust. (6–10)

Antony himself acknowledges what Philo has said in the very next
scene: "These strong Egyptian fetters I must break / Or lose myself in
dotage" (1.2.117–18). Doting, or being excessively fond, is a particular
problem of the old. Idleness is, too, which Antony takes up a few lines
later:

I must from this enchanting queen break off:
Ten thousand harms, more than the ills I know,
My idleness doth hatch. (129–31)

Idleness means both indolence and foolishness. The word is particularly important in this play. As Antony bitterly exclaims, Cleopatra is
the queen of idleness:

But that your royalty
Holds idleness your subject, I should take you
For idleness itself. (1.3.91–93)

Idleness here conveys negative connotations of triviality and frivolity.
   The aging Antony is acutely conscious of becoming anonymous
and invisible. This is a problem that recurs in all of Shakespeare's history plays. Richard II, deposed by Bolingbroke, has become "a mockery
king of snow" (4.1.259) who laments his present status:

I have no name, no title,
No, not that name was given me at the font
But 'tis usurped. (254–56)

In a passage that seems to echo the dialogue between Hamlet and Polonius (3.2.382–94) and is recalled in Prospero's revels speech in *The
Tempest* (4.1.148–58), Antony expatiates with Eros, his fellow soldier,
about the unstable cloud shapes that symbolize his fateful decline:

That which is now a horse, even with a thought
The rack dislimns, and makes it indistinct
As water is in water. (4.14.9–11)

The last line offers an extraordinary image of deliquescence, like Antipholus of Syracuse's quest for his missing twin in *The Comedy of Errors*:

I to the world am like a drop of water
That in the ocean seeks another drop,
Who, falling there to find his fellow forth,
Unseen, inquisitive, confounds himself. (1.2.35–38)

As he contemplates his end, Antony becomes meditative and lyrical,
comparing himself to the shifting cloud shapes: "Here I am Antony, /
Yet cannot hold this visible shape" (4.14.13–14). In his first soliloquy
Hamlet, too, wishes that his "sullied flesh would melt, / Thaw, and resolve itself into a dew" (1.2.129–30).

"Dislimns" is an odd word used only once in Shakespeare. Since
"limn" is what an artist does when he paints a picture, "dislimn" means
to erase an image. There is wordplay on "rack" (4.14.10), which can either refer to clouds or to an instrument of torture, which stretches
and pulls apart a person's joints. This is the sense of "dislimbs" noted in
the Arden edition.[2] The word is part of a curious concentration of "dis"
prefix words that characterize Antony's fall and eventual death: "dislimn," "discandying" (3.13.165), "discandy" (4.12.22), "disponge" (4.9.13),
"discomfort" (4.2.34), "dissuade" (4.6.13), and "dissolve" (5.2.299). They
form part of the central imagery of melting, which traces Antony's
descent. It begins with Antony's line "Authority melts from me"
(3.13.90), when he cannot prevent Thidias, Caesar's servant, from kiss-
ing Cleopatra's hand. It ends when Antony dies and Cleopatra exclaims:
"The crown o' th' earth doth melt" (4.15.63). Some of these terms are
hapax legomena, words used only once in Shakespeare, and remain
unique to this play.

Antony's unarming plays out his dissolution and fall. It begins right
after he has heard the news of Cleopatra's death from Mardian, her

eunuch—a false report, of course, intended to give her additional time to deal with her lover's anger. Antony immediately asks his fellow soldier Eros to disarm him as if he is preparing for death: "Unarm, Eros. The long day's task is done, / And we must sleep" (4.14.35–36). Like Othello, his reputation is destroyed, and now, without his armor, he is "no more a soldier" (42). He longs to overtake Cleopatra in an imagined Elysium. The famous lovers Dido and Aeneas "shall want troops, / And all the haunt be ours" (53–54). Antony pleads with Eros to kill him, but Eros kills himself instead. Antony falls on his own sword, but he only wounds himself. He then earnestly requests that Diomedes give him "sufficing strokes for death" (117), but Diomedes demurs and announces that Cleopatra is alive. In the face of what could be the final proof of Cleopatra's treachery, Antony has no reaction. He only wishes to be brought to her in her monument and to die quickly. Antony's movement in these last scenes is like a final melting and lyrical disappearance. His rage is totally forgotten.

In an earlier scene Cleopatra tries—unsuccessfully—to help Antony put on his armor. Antony politely protests: "Ah, let be, let be! Thou art / The armorer of my heart. False, false; this, this" (4.6.6–7). Following his defeat at the battle of Actium, Antony feels as if he is entering the darkness of night and death: "I am so lated in the world that I / Have lost my way forever" (3.11.3–4). "Lated" means belated, as of a traveler overtaken by darkness. In act 3, scene 3, of *Macbeth* the three murderers are waiting to kill Banquo and Fleance. The first murderer seems to be speaking about their approach:

> Now spurs the lated traveler apace
> To gain the timely inn, and near approaches
> The subject of our watch. (6–8)

In a key moment in act 3, scene 11, the stage direction states that Antony *"sits down"* (24), as if to symbolize his present lowly status. Then Cleopatra enters with Eros and her attendants Charmian and Iras and asks to sit down, too, but Antony violently protests: "No, no, no, no, no" (29).

Why is Antony so agitated here? He rebukes himself for his own passivity in following Cleopatra's ships and fleeing from the battle:

> Egypt, thou knew'st too well
> My heart was to thy rudder tied by th' strings,
> And thou shouldst tow me after. (56–58)

The essence of the matter lies in Antony's tragic conflict: his military prowess, symbolized by his sword, is "made weak" by his "affection" (67). This is the reason Enobarbus deserts him:

> When valor preys on reason,
> It eats the sword it fights with. I will seek
> Some way to leave him. (3.13.199–201)

In the end Enobarbus is saying what Antony himself knows only too well.

11. POWERFUL OLDER WOMEN

There are many powerful older women in Shakespeare's works. The question arises as to how we know they are old. In Shakespeare's time men were generally considered old at around fifty, whereas women were thought to be old when they were no longer capable of having children. Thus, one may speculate that post-menopausal women were in their mid- to late forties. This works out to a ten-year difference between old men and women. These are, of course, very general figures subject to a great many exceptions.

One obvious example of a powerful woman is Volumnia in *Coriolanus*.[1] Although her age is never specified, she is a grandmother at the beginning of the play. She is a very authoritarian figure, and she brings up her son, Marcius (later called Coriolanus) to be a heroic warrior. This becomes obvious very early in the play. In a domestic scene between the two women, Volumnia expresses her military values to Virgilia, the wife of Marcius, who is tender-hearted and frightened of the risks her husband runs in battle. When Volumnia speaks of her son's "bloody brow" (1.3.37), she manages to scare her daughter-in-law: "His bloody brow? O Jupiter, no blood!" (41). This only encourages Volumnia's gory rhetoric:

> Away, you fool! It more becomes a man
> Than gilt his trophy. The breasts of Hecuba,
> When she did suckle Hector, looked not lovelier
> Than Hector's forehead when it spit forth blood
> At Grecian sword, contemning. (42–46)

This echoes Lady Macbeth's ferocious assertion to "unsex" (1.5.42) her femininity in order to persuade her husband to murder King Duncan. She would have plucked the nipple from the "boneless gums" of her nursing babe and dashed its brains out if she had sworn to commit the murder as she is convinced her husband has. This is just one of many similarities between Lady Macbeth and Volumnia.

Volumnia reasserts her manly, militaristic values in the second act when Menenius, the old aristocratic counselor, asks if Marcius is wounded, as if this is a certain mark of his valor: "Is he wounded? He was wont to come home wounded" (2.1.122–23). Virgilia is again frightened: "O, no, no, no" (124). Volumnia, however, is triumphant: "O, he is wounded; I thank the gods for't" (125). Marcius's mother is preoccupied with her son's wounds throughout the scene. She is ecstatic when she hears the news and asks: "True? Pow waw!" (147). This unusual exclamation doesn't occur anywhere else in Shakespeare. She enumerates her son's previous twenty-five battle wounds, which now number twenty-seven. She announces rather grandly the arrival of her son on the scene:

> Before him he carries noise, and behind him he leaves tears.
> Death, that dark spirit, in's nervy [sinewy] arm doth lie,
> Which, being advanced, declines, and then men die. (164–67)

The celebration of death is obviously disturbing to Virgilia, but she is the only one who doesn't share in Volumnia's heroic, aristocratic values.

When Coriolanus encounters difficulties in winning the people's votes in order to become consul, Volumnia tries to persuade her son to be "politic" (3.2.42). In other words, he must temporarily suspend his heroic values and be crafty and circumspect in order to win over the rabble and their elected tribunes. This is a central conflict in the play, since Volumnia is the source of these heroic values and is now telling her son to dissemble for political gain. She provides precise instructions concerning the role he is to play, treating him as if he were a child:

> I prithee now, my son,
> Go to them [the Roman people] with this bonnet in thy hand;
> And thus far having stretched it (here be with them),
> Thy knee bussing [kissing] the stones (for in such business
> Action is eloquence, and the eyes of th' ignorant
> More learned than the ears), waving thy head,
> Which often thus correcting thy stout heart,
> Now humble as the ripest mulberry
> That will not hold the handling. (72–80)

Volumnia's lengthy speech ends with the splendid image of an overripe mulberry. Perhaps Volumnia's instructions are so tediously detailed because she has to convince not only her son but herself of what she is saying.

This is obviously what her son thinks, and the more his mother says the less he seems convinced. He explicitly states that what his mother is saying goes against all his—and her—heroic values:

> Must I
> With my base tongue give to my noble heart
> A lie that it must bear? (99–101)

Volumnia only thinks in terms of compulsion: "He must, and will. / Prithee now, say you will, and go about it" (97–98). Of course, Coriolanus cannot play the humble role advocated by his mother. He is incapable of dissembling in order to become consul. In the end, he remains true to himself and is banished.

When the exiled Coriolanus joins with his enemy Aufidius and threatens to capture and destroy his native city, a final deputation from Rome pleads with him to spare the city. His mother is the chief pleader, but before she even begins to speak we sense that Coriolanus is vulnerable when he says:

> My mother bows,
> As if Olympus to a molehill should
> In supplication nod. (5.3.29–31)

Although Coriolanus steels himself to

> stand
> As if a man were author of himself
> And knew no other kin (36–38),

we know that he will not be able to withstand his mother's supplication. Volumnia even threatens to commit suicide should her embassy prove unsuccessful:

> If I can not persuade thee
> Rather to show a noble grace to both parts [parties to the war]
> Than seek the end of one, thou shalt no sooner
> March to assault thy country than to tread
> (Trust to't, thou shalt not) on thy mother's womb
> That brought thee to this world. (120–25)

After several lengthy speeches there is a sudden break in the discourse and the stage direction reads: *"Holds her by the hand, silent"* (182). This is one of the most eloquent nonverbal gestures in all of Shakespeare. It is decisive, and Coriolanus realizes that he has just sealed his own fate:

Behold, the heavens do ope,
The gods look down, and this unnatural scene
They laugh at. O my mother, mother! O!
You have won a happy victory to Rome;
But, for your son—believe it, O, believe it!—
Most dangerously you have with him prevailed,
If not most mortal to him. (183–89)

This unnatural scene—a mother pleading with her errant son—is clearly fateful for Coriolanus. This sacrifice of her son seems to be what Volumnia wanted all along, going far beyond her praise of the wounds he has received in battle. Willing to abandon her own and her son's honor in order to save Rome, Volumnia has made a tragic choice.

Queen Margaret, the widow of King Henry VI, appears in the *Henry VI* plays, but by the time of *Richard III*, the fourth play in the tetralogy, she is old and querulous.[2] One remembers her savage cruelty in *3 Henry VI,* when the Duke of York, thinking of his son's murder, calls her "she-wolf of France" (1.4.111) and exclaims: "O tiger's heart wrapped in a woman's hide!" (137). This phrase is recalled from Robert Greene's parody in his final attack on Shakespeare: "Tygers hart wrapt in a Players hide."[3] In act I, scene 3 of *Richard III*, she enters from behind while Richard is speaking scornfully to Queen Elizabeth (Lady Grey), the wife of King Edward IV. Queen Margaret expresses a bitter aside to counter the claims of Richard and Queen Elizabeth. As an addendum to Richard's speech, she tells the audience:

Out, devil! I do remember them too well.
Thou kill'dst my husband Henry in the Tower
And Edward, my poor son, at Tewkesbury. (117–19)

An old woman, she functions as the voice of memory to remind Richard of his heinous deeds on the way to the throne (he is not yet king). When Richard hypocritically remarks, "I am too childish-foolish for this world" (141), Margaret's aside underscores his clever cultivation of false appearances: "Hie thee to hell for shame and leave this world, / Thou cacodemon [evil spirit]! There thy kingdom is" (142–43). When she can bear no more, she steps forward and continues to rail against all those present:

> Which of you trembles not that looks on me?
> If not, that I am queen, you bow like subjects,
> Yet that, by you deposed, you quake like rebels. (159–61)

Later the deposed King Richard II will sound like Margaret, but Richard of Gloucester feels only contempt: "Foul wrinkled witch, what mak'st thou in my sight?" (163). Richard already speaks as if he were king.

Richard calls Margaret "thou hateful withered hag" (214), but this does not stop her from spewing her litany of doom. She curses him and predicts his downfall:

> No sleep close up that deadly eye of thine,
> Unless it be while some tormenting dream
> Affrights thee with a hell of ugly devils! (224–26)

This actually occurs when the ghosts appear to Richard before the battle of Bosworth Field (5.3). Margaret doesn't tire of cursing Richard and points to his physical deformity as a mark of his evil nature:

> Thou elvish-marked, abortive, rooting hog!
> Thou that wast sealed in thy nativity
> The slave of nature and the son of hell!
> Thou slander of thy heavy mother's womb!
> Thou loathèd issue of thy father's loins! (227–31)

Richard seems unperturbed—even amused—by Margaret's vehement denunciations.

In the balance of the play Queen Margaret functions as a kind of Cassandra figure, predicting future woes. This is especially true in her counsel to Buckingham to beware of Richard:

O Buckingham, take heed of yonder dog!
Look when he fawns he bites; and when he bites,
His venom tooth will rankle to the death. (1.3.288–90)

In her exit speech she warns Buckingham of his inevitable doom:

O, but remember this another day,
When he shall split thy very heart with sorrow,
And say poor Margaret was a prophetess. (298–300)

In the scene involving the fall of Buckingham, he remembers Margaret's words:

Thus Margaret's curse falls heavy on my neck:
"When he," quoth she, "shall split thy heart with sorrow,
Remember Margaret was a prophetess."
Come lead me, officers, to the block of shame. (5.1.25–28)

Throughout the play Margaret functions as a kind of arbiter of history, setting the record straight for Richard and his henchmen.

In an elegiac scene Queen Margaret grieves with Queen Elizabeth, whose husband (King Edward IV) and sons Richard has murdered, and with the Duchess of York, Richard's mother. As the scene opens she expresses her satisfaction at the outcome of her revenge:

Here in these confines slily have I lurked
To watch the waning of mine enemies. (4.4.3–4)

She retires and speaks in an aside as the Duchess of York and Queen Elizabeth enter. When she comes forward, she rhapsodically describes the tragedies of all three women in succession, beginning with herself:

I had an Edward [her son], till a Richard killed him;
I had a husband [King Henry VI], till a Richard killed him.
    (40–41)

Next she addresses Queen Elizabeth:

> Thou hadst an Edward [her husband and son], till a Richard
>   killed him;
> Thou hadst a Richard [her son], till a Richard killed him. (42–43)

Then she turns to the Duchess of York:

> From forth the kennel of thy womb hath crept
> A hellhound that doth hunt us all to death.
> That dog that had his teeth before his eyes,
> To worry lambs and lap their gentle blood. (47–50)

Queen Margaret seems to delight in the consequences of her role as avenging chorus: "I am hungry for revenge, / And now I cloy me with beholding it" (61–62). "Cloy" implies an excess, as in overeating. She prays greedily for Richard's death:

> Earth gapes, hell burns, fiends roar, saints pray,
> To have him suddenly conveyed from hence.
> Cancel his bond of life, dear God, I pray,
> That I may live and say, "The dog is dead." (75–78)

There is a certain tediousness in this scene as Margaret's maledictions seem to go on forever. This is clearly an early history play; the later history plays are leaner and more pointed.

The Duchess of York, the mother of Richard of Gloucester (later King Richard III), is a grieving woman very much like Queen Margaret. Her age is specifically identified: "Eighty odd years of sorrow have I seen" (4.1.95). By act 2, scene 2, Richard has already murdered his brothers, Edward and Clarence. The old Duchess of York enters the scene with Clarence's two children. She agrees that their uncle lied to them about the death of their father, and she tries to distance herself from her son:

Ah, that deceit should steal such gentle shape
And with a virtuous visor hide deep vice!
He is my son, ay, and therein my shame;
Yet from my dugs he drew not this deceit. (27–30)

When Richard enters, he begs his mother's blessing, but when she gives it, he voices a sardonic aside: "And make me die a good old man! / This is the butt-end of a mother's blessing" (109–10). Later the Duchess of York competes with Queen Margaret and Queen Elizabeth in terms of their grieving, as if none of the three can bear to be outdone. When her son Richard enters, she is fierce in her curses:

O, she that might have intercepted thee,
By strangling thee in her accursèd womb,
From all the slaughters, wretch, that thou hast done! (137–39)

She addresses her son as "thou toad" (145), but Richard calls for a trumpet flourish so that these tattling women will not be able to "rail on the Lord's anointed" (151).

However, the Duchess of York will not be silenced. She recounts Richard's career, beginning with his difficult birth and childhood:

Thou cam'st on earth to make the earth my hell.
A grievous burden was thy birth to me;
Tetchy and wayward was thy infancy;
Thy schooldays frightful, desp'rate, wild, and furious;
Thy prime of manhood daring, bold, and venturous;
Thy age confirmed, proud, subtle, sly, and bloody. (167–72)

Richard parries her words with irony. He doesn't answer any of her accusations, as if they were all too trivial for comment. His mother's final words before she exits are in the form of a bitter curse: "Bloody thou art, bloody will be thy end; / Shame serves thy life and doth thy death attend" (195–96).

It is interesting that Shakespeare uses all three grieving queens to provide a moral commentary on Richard, nor is there any attempt to conceal his evildoing. Everything is laid out plainly by Richard himself, especially in his soliloquies, as well as in the accusations of the three queens. The fact that Queen Margaret and the Duchess of York are old lends gravity to their words. The strongest moral figure is Richard's mother, and her curses give a special edge to the scene. One thinks of Lear cursing Goneril: "How sharper than a serpent's tooth it is / To have a thankless child" (1.4.280–81).

Queen Gertrude in *Hamlet* is not given any specific age in the play, but in the closet scene Hamlet speaks of his mother as menopausal:[4]

> You cannot call it love, for at your age
> The heyday in the blood is tame, it's humble,
> And waits upon the judgment. (3.4.69–71)

The blood is the source of sexual desire in Renaissance physiology, and it was generally believed that following menopause sexual desire lessened and passion was subordinated to reason ("judgment"). This is, of course, not a specific reference to Gertrude's age, but she is definitely beyond her childbearing years. There is a contradiction between Hamlet's statement that the heyday of his mother's blood is "tame, it's humble" and his many references to her energetic pursuit of sexual activity:

> Nay, but to live
> In the rank sweat of an enseamèd bed,
> Stewed in corruption, honeying and making love
> Over the nasty sty. (92–95)

A possible explanation is that at Gertrude's age the heyday in her blood *should* be tame and humble but isn't. There was a general feeling in the Renaissance that vigorous sexual activity was harmful to the health of old people, who were naturally cold and dry.

Gertrude remains a commanding figure in the closet scene until Hamlet's revelations break her resolution. She begins with the clear intention of upbraiding her son for his outrageous conduct: "Hamlet, thou hast thy father [Claudius] much offended" (10). Believing that his mother is complicit in his father's murder, Hamlet responds sarcastically: "Mother, you have my father much offended" (11). Gertrude is still imperious in her reply: "Come, come, you answer with an idle tongue" (13). She insists that Hamlet maintain the respect due his mother, asking: "Have you forgot me?" (15). However, her son is still on the attack: "You are the Queen, your husband's brother's wife, / And, would it were not so, you are my mother" (16–17). Gertrude has grown increasingly angry at the unexpected turn things have taken—her son is not at all repentant for his conduct—and corrects him as one would a small child: "Nay, then I'll set those to you that can speak" (18). This is a hint to Polonius, who is hiding behind the arras. Undaunted, Hamlet becomes more aggressive and forces his mother to sit down while he drives home his accusations: "You go not till I set you up a glass / Where you may see the inmost part of you!" (20–21). Gertrude, fearing for her life— "Thou wilt not murder me?" (22)—calls for help. Polonius cries out from behind the arras and is immediately stabbed by Hamlet: "Dead for a ducat, dead!" (25).

I think we are meant to believe that there is a good chance that Hamlet might murder his mother, as he indicates in the soliloquy that ends act 3, scene 2. He steels himself to follow the Ghost's injunction— "Leave her to heaven" (1.5.86)—as he prepares to visit his mother in her closet, but it is difficult for him to be so resolute:

> O heart, lose not thy nature; let not ever
> The soul of Nero [who had his mother murdered] enter this
>   firm bosom.
> Let me be cruel, not unnatural;
> I will speak daggers to her, but use none. (3.2.401–4)

This soliloquy clearly anticipates how the beginning of the closet scene is to be played: Hamlet is definitely intending to speak bluntly.

Hamlet's homicidal mood doesn't break until right after the death of Polonius, when he accuses his mother of murder. She exclaims: "O, what a rash and bloody deed is this!" (28), to which Hamlet counters with: "A bloody deed—almost as bad, good Mother, / As kill a king, and marry with his brother" (29–30). The queen is startled by this accusation—"As kill a king?" (31)—and this seems to end the idea that she participated in her late husband's murder. From this point on Hamlet speaks only of his mother's moral guilt, and she becomes progressively more humble and conscience-stricken: "O Hamlet, thou hast cleft my heart in twain" (157).

The fact that Gertrude doesn't see the Ghost is not, I think, an indication of her coarseness of feeling but rather an Elizabethan stage convention concerning ghosts. Lady Macbeth likewise doesn't see the ghost of Banquo in *Macbeth* (3.4). As the Ghost prepares to exit, Hamlet asks Gertrude: "Do you see nothing there?" (3.4.132), to which the queen answers simply: "Nothing at all; yet all that is I see" (133). Hamlet is astonished, whereas the queen believes that her son must be mad:

> This is the very coinage of your brain.
> This bodiless creation ecstasy
> Is very cunning in. (138–40)

Hamlet assures his mother that he is not mad, and a very sorrowful Gertrude convinces him that she will keep his secret:

> Be thou assured, if words be made of breath,
> And breath of life, I have no life to breathe
> What thou hast said to me. (198–200)

This secret is confirmed in the next scene, when Gertrude tells Claudius that her son—"mad as the sea and wind when both contend / Which is the mightier" (4.1.7–8)—has killed Polonius. She is firmly allied with her son and even speaks of Hamlet's unlikely remorse: "'A weeps for what is done" (27).

It is interesting that Claudius, in an effort to win over the rebellious Laertes, explains why he has not proceeded directly against Hamlet.

One of the reasons is the great attachment between himself and Gertrude:

> She is so conjunctive to my life and soul,
> That, as the star moves not but in his sphere,
> I could not but by her. (4.7.14–16)

What are we to make of this? Is the wily Claudius merely trying to win Laertes over or does he really mean it? There is no way to know for sure, but in the final scene of the play Claudius does not snatch the cup from Gertrude's hand when she begins to drink from the poisoned chalice. He says only: "Gertrude, do not drink" (5.2.291). The queen is faithful to her son to the last and warns him: "O my dear Hamlet! / The drink, the drink! I am poisoned" (310–11). Just before Gertrude drinks from the poisoned cup, there is a tender moment when she says to her sweating son: "Here, Hamlet, take my napkin, rub thy brows" (289).

In "The Mousetrap" play-within-a-play the Player Queen is usually understood to be a stand-in for Gertrude. Hamlet attacks her sanctimonious insistence that she will never marry again:

> The instances that second marriage move
> Are base respects of thrift, but none of love.
> A second time I kill my husband dead
> When second husband kisses me in bed. (3.2.188–91)

This leads to the issue of Gertrude's incest, upon which the Ghost vehemently insists. When Hamlet asks his mother: "Madam, how like you this play?" (235), she answers with withering skepticism: "The lady doth protest too much, methinks" (236). Gertrude clearly wants to separate herself from the platitudinous Player Queen. There is great ambiguity surrounding Gertrude's role in the play—even more so than Hamlet's—since we never really learn about her relations with Claudius while her husband was still alive, having only the Ghost's accusations to go by.

The Witches and Hecate in *Macbeth* are examples of other powerful old women. It is quite clear that they are old. Hecate calls them "beldams" (3.5.2), or hags, and Macbeth addresses them as "you secret, black, and midnight hags" (4.1.48) and, later, as "filthy hags" (115). Banquo tells the Witches:

> You seem to understand me,
> By each at once her choppy [chapped] finger laying
> Upon her skinny lips. (1.3.43–45)

They are women with male characteristics, as Banquo further elaborates:

> You should be women,
> And yet your beards forbid me to interpret
> That you are so. (45–47)

In other words, they are monstrous creatures, "weïrd sisters" (32), as they refer to themselves and as they are called by Macbeth and Banquo throughout the play. "Weird" is derived from the Anglo-Saxon *wyrd*, meaning fate, and the weird sisters function as the three Fates in the play. Nothing specific is said to characterize Hecate separately, but she is clearly in charge of the weird sisters, who have only limited powers. For the sailor, "master o' th' Tiger" (1.3.7), who is to Aleppo gone, the First Witch can only deprive him of sleep:

> Weary sev'nights nine time nine
> Shall he dwindle, peak, and pine:
> Though his bark cannot be lost,
> Yet it shall be tempest-tossed. (22–25)

The Witches are "juggling fiends" (5.8.19), as Macbeth acknowledges, but they cannot either determine or alter his fate.

12. LOVING OLDER WOMEN

Volumnia in *Coriolanus* is hardly a loving mother. When she persuades her son to spare Rome, she is directly responsible for his death. Gertrude in *Hamlet* is an ambiguous character. In the closet scene (3.4) she may prove loving in the end, but the scene doesn't begin that way. Hamlet may not be entirely convinced that his mother was not complicit in his father's death.

There are a number of loving mothers and wives in Shakespeare, of whom the most ideal example is the Countess of Rousillon in *All's Well That Ends Well*. She is a tender, loving mother—or surrogate mother—to Helena, the daughter of the late physician Gerard de Narbon, and she is much concerned about what happens to Bertram, her unworthy son. She is called *"Old Lady"* in the opening stage directions of acts 4 and 5. When her steward reports that he overheard Helena speak of her love for Bertram, the countess says in an aside: "Even so it was with me, when I was young" (1.3.130). Obviously she is no longer young. In a plea for sympathy for her love affair, Helena speaks of the countess's "agèd honor" (212). In her witty dialogue with the Clown the countess wishes "to be young again, if we could" (2.2.39). But in the amusing exchange between Parolles and the Clown, the countess is clearly identified by Parolles as "my old lady" (2.4.19). The Clown's reply emphasizes her old age: "So that you had her wrinkles and I her money, I would she did as you say" (20–21).

The play begins with the death of the Countess of Rousillon's husband. She recalls almost immediately the death of Helena's father, Gerard de Narbon, a famous physician who has entrusted his only child to the countess's "overlooking" (1.1.41). The word means guardianship, but it also indicates wardship, as Bertram is the ward of the king. The countess generously praises Helena:

> I have those hopes of her good that her education promises; her dispositions she inherits, which makes fair gifts fairer . . . she derives [inherits] her honesty and achieves her goodness. (41–43, 47–48) .

She expands these loving sentiments later in act 1:

> Her father bequeathed her to me, and she herself, without other advantage, may lawfully make title to as much love as she finds. There is more owing to her than is paid, and more shall be paid her than she'll demand. (1.3.102–6)

"Advantage" means interest paid on borrowed money, as in *The Merchant of Venice* when Shylock says that Antonio claims to "neither lend nor borrow / Upon advantage" (1.3.66–67). This clearly indicates the countess's boundless love: "More shall be paid to her than she'll demand."

Later in the same scene the countess addresses Helena directly: "You know, Helen, / I am a mother to you" (139–40), a claim that worries Helena because she is in love with Bertram, the countess's son, and fears the imputation of incest. The countess, however, is fully aware of

Helena's anxieties. She doesn't permit Helena to address her as "Mine honorable mistress" (141):

> Nay, a mother.
> Why not a mother? When I said "a mother"
> Methought you saw a serpent. What's in "mother"
> That you start at it? I say I am your mother,
> And put you in the catalogue of those
> That were enwombèd mine. (141–46)

The Countess insists on her maternal relation to Helena:

> You ne'er oppressed me with a mother's groan,
> Yet I express to you a mother's care. (149–50)

"Daughter" also meant "daughter-in-law" in Shakespeare's time, but this is the only play that actually uses the word "daughter-in-law" (three times, in fact), which provides the solution to Helena's fears. The countess relieves Helena's anxieties about the word "mother" when she declares:

> Yes, Helen, you might be my daughter-in-law.
> God shield [forbid] you mean it not! "Daughter" and "mother"
> So strive upon your pulse! (169–71)

So the countess ministers very solicitously to Helena's emotional needs.

With her son, Bertram, the countess blesses him at his leave taking in a manner very similar to the scene between Polonius and Laertes (*Hamlet,* 1.3):

> Be thou blessed, Bertram, and succeed thy father
> In manners as in shape! Thy blood and virtue
> Contend for empire in thee, and thy goodness
> Share with thy birthright! (1.1.65–68)

She offers semiproverbial and epigrammatic precepts that echo Polonius's more didactic and much longer moral disquisition:

> Love all, trust a few,
> Do wrong to none; be able for thine enemy
> Rather in power than use, and keep thy friend
> Under thy own life's key. Be checked for silence,
> But never taxed for speech. (68–72)

Although the countess is not tedious the way Polonius is, both express their loving concerns for their sons.

The countess is genuinely shocked by Bertram's strange absconding from his wife, Helena, and his riddling letter to her. Her immediate reaction is to renounce him:

> He was my son,
> But I do wash his name out of my blood
> And thou art all my child. (3.2.68–70)

She flatters Helena, who

> deserves a lord
> That twenty such rude boys might tend upon
> And call her, hourly, mistress. (83–85)

The countess attributes her son's strange behavior to the bad counsel of Parolles, whose "inducement" "corrupts" Bertram's "well-derivèd nature" (91). The countess's concern for her puts Helena in a difficult position, and it is at this point that she decides to leave for Florence in disguise and seek a more practical way to win her husband back.

The countess, for her part, is eager for Helena's return, and seeks a way to have her reconciled with her husband. It is clear that her renunciation of her son was only a petulant reaction to his letter. She is still the ever-loving mother, as she subsequently declares so movingly:

> Which of them both
> Is dearest to me, I have no skill in sense
> To make distinction. (3.4.38–40)

She writes an earnest letter to Bertram in which she declares Helena's worth: "Let every word weigh heavy of her worth / That he does weigh too light" (31–32). The countess falsely assumes that Helena and her son will return at her earnest entreaty. She is already anticipating a happy ending, but it turns out to be more bittersweet than the countess imagines.

We do not see her again until later in the play, where she mourns over the purported death of Helena: "It was the death of the most virtuous gentlewoman that ever nature had praise for creating. If she had partaken of my flesh and cost me the dearest groans of a mother, I could not have owed her a more rooted love" (4.5.8–13). In the final scene of the play the countess forgives her son for the suffering he has caused, which she attributes to his youthful years:

> Natural rebellion done i' th' blade [green shoot] of youth,
> When oil and fire, too strong for reason's force,
> O'erbears it and burns on. (5.3.6–8)

The audience—and readers—don't usually forgive the problematic Bertram as easily as his mother does. In the final working out of the plot the countess has very little to say. Her role as loving reconciler is preempted by the Widow, the mother of Diana (whom Bertram is trying to seduce). She is also an older woman.

In the second part of *The Winter's Tale*, after the sixteen-year gap in time, Hermione is obviously much older than she was earlier in the play. Paulina, who has preserved Hermione's life, makes an esthetic point about the wrinkles of the statue, which are a proof of Julio Romano's skill,

our carver's excellence,
Which lets go by some sixteen years, and makes her
As she lived now. (5.3.30–32)

So the statue is the portrait of a convincingly older woman. The love speeches are almost entirely delivered by Leontes, the long-suffering and now repentant husband. Hermione doesn't come alive until about line 103, when Paulina says: "You perceive she stirs." Leontes affirms that "she's warm" (109). Hermione embraces him and "hangs about his neck" (112), but she doesn't speak until she hears from Paulina that "Our Perdita is found" (121).

It's interesting that Hermione has only one speech in this crucial scene, whereas we expect her to say much more. She doesn't say a word to her husband; her speech is entirely addressed to her newfound daughter:

You gods look down,
And from your sacred vials pour your graces
Upon my daughter's head! (121–23)

Hermione considers the whole scene not so much proof of Paulina's ingenuity in preserving her but of the beneficence of providence. It is a proof of the grace of the gods.

Her curiosity is entirely concerned with Perdita rather than Leontes:

Tell me, mine own,
Where hast thou been preserved? Where lived? How found
Thy father's court? For thou shalt hear that I,
Knowing by Paulina that the oracle
Gave hope thou wast in being, have preserved
Myself to see the issue. (123–28)

There is more than a hint here that Hermione has preserved her life solely to be reunited with her daughter. Her speech has acting implica-

tions for her behavior toward Leontes. It would appear that he is ecstatic over the reunion, whereas she is not.

Paulina plays a very loving role in ministering to Hermione and in
insisting that Leontes endure his penance to the end and not marry
again. The opening of act 5 prepares us for the reappearance of Hermione in the final scene. Paulina insists on Hermione's perfection and
wants to make sure that Leontes never forgets it:

> If one by one you wedded all the world,
> Or from the all that are took something good
> To make a perfect woman, she you killed
> Would be unparalleled. (5.1.13–16)

Leontes is stung by the words "she you killed," which bolsters his resolve never to remarry. Paulina insists that it is all the will of the gods:

> Besides, the gods
> Will have fulfilled their secret purposes;
> For has not the divine Apollo said—
> Is 't not the tenor of his oracle—
> That King Leontes shall not have an heir
> Till his lost child be found? (35–40)

In these portentous passages she speaks like a priestess of the gods.
The sacred oracle hangs over the reappearance of Hermione, whom
Leontes calls a "sainted spirit" (57).

Paulina cleverly gets Leontes to agree never to marry

> unless another,
> As like Hermione as is her picture,
> Affront his eye. (73–75)

This proviso makes it evident that Hermione will definitely reappear.
Paulina prepares for the statue scene by providing loving detail. She
begs Leontes to give her the office

To choose you a queen; she shall not be so young
As was your former, but she shall be such
As, walked your first queen's ghost, it should take joy
To see her in your arms. (5.1.78–81)

We are thus prepared for the wrinkled appearance of Hermione of
act 5, scene 3! The reappearance of Perdita at the end of this scene sets
the stage for the revivification of her mother. Their fates seem to be
intertwined.

Katherine of Aragon, the wife of King Henry VIII in the play of
the same name, is another example of a compassionate, loving older
women. She confesses to Cardinal Wolsey that the king

Alas, has banished me his bed already;
His love, too long ago! I am old, my lords,
And all the fellowship I hold now with him
Is only my obedience. (3.1.119–22)

The historical Katherine, born in 1485, was forty-three at the time. The
opening stage direction for act 4, scene 2, reads: *"Enter Katherine, Dowa-
ger, sick,"* and by the end of the scene she is near death.

Her trial scene (2.4) echoes the trial of Hermione in *The Winter's Tale*
(3.2). In both we are meant to experience great compassion for the loving heroines. Katherine appeals to the king, but the trial is conducted by
her enemies, cardinals Wolsey and Campeius. She asks her husband:

Alas, sir,
In what have I offended you? What cause
Hath my behavior given to your displeasure
That thus you should proceed to put me off
And take your good grace from me? (18–22)

There is, of course, no cause except the king's dynastic ambitions, as
well as his sudden affection for the much younger Anne Bullen.

Katherine's eloquent speech fills us with compassion for her, a woman wrongfully accused and shamefully treated:

> Sir, call to mind
> That I have been your wife in this obedience
> Upward of twenty years, and have been blessed
> With many children by you. If, in the course
> And process of this time, you can report,
> And prove it too, against mine honor aught,
> My bond to wedlock or my love and duty,
> Against your sacred person, in God's name,
> Turn me away. (34–42)

Katherine speaks with a convincing simplicity and sincerity.

Of course, the king completely agrees with her. In a moving declaration right after Katherine exits, he speaks of her as a nonpareil of a loving wife:

> If thy rare qualities, sweet gentleness,
> Thy meekness saint-like, wife-like government,
> Obeying in commanding, and thy parts
> Sovereign and pious else, could speak thee out—
> The queen of earthly queens. (137–41)

Yet all of these qualities do nothing to change the king's mind, who is determined to marry Anne Bullen.

Katherine is presented very sympathetically in a domestic scene in act 3, scene 1. The opening stage direction reads: *"Enter Queen and her Women, as at work."* She is not eager to speak with Wolsey and Campeius, whom she considers her sworn enemies: "What can be their business / With me, a poor weak woman, fall'n from favor?" (19–20). She speaks of herself as a humble "housewife" (24), and she asks Wolsey to speak in English, not Latin. She points to the inappropriateness of the context:

> I was set [seated] at work
> Among my maids, full little, God knows, looking
> Either for such men or such business. (74–76)

She turns a deaf ear to their false persuasions:

> Is this your comfort?
> The cordial that ye bring a wretched lady,
> A woman lost among ye, laughed at, scorned?
> I will not wish ye half my miseries:
> I have more charity. (105–9)

Katherine is noble and remains devoted to the king even in her downfall. We feel her grief intensely. Her spotless innocence is expressed in the image of the lily, familiar from devotional texts:

> Like the lily,
> That once was mistress of the field, and flourished,
> I'll hang my head and perish. (151–53)

In her final scene Katherine is "sick to death. / My legs like loaden branches bow to th' earth" (4.2.1–2). Following the stage direction *"Sad and solemn music"* (80), Katherine sleeps and there is a beautiful, masque-like *"Vision"* of "Spirits of peace" (83) that look forward to her beatific end. Her last words are spoken to Lord Capucius, the ambassador from the emperor:

> I was a chaste wife to my grave. Embalm me,
> Then lay me forth. Although unqueened, yet like
> A queen and daughter to a king, inter me.
> I can [can do] no more. (170–73)

Katherine exits the play as a kind of martyr. The old, foreign queen—she is Katherine of Aragon, the same country as one of Portia's suitors in *The Merchant of Venice*—goes to her death guiltless and innocent.

Another nurturant woman is the abbess in *The Comedy of Errors*. At the end of the play she says:

Thirty-three years have I but gone in travail
Of you, my sons, and till this present hour
My heavy burden ne'er delivered. (5.1.401–3)

Editors have puzzled over those thirty-three years since the shipwreck, which are inconsistent with other enumerations in the play, but Emilia, wife of Egeon, is clearly an old lady at this point. Her unknown son, Antipholus of Syracuse, has taken refuge in her priory, but she steadfastly refuses to give up the "poor distracted husband" to his wife, Adriana. The abbess acts as a psychological counselor to Antipholus, accusing Adriana of driving him to distraction:

The venom clamors of a jealous woman
Poisons more deadly than a mad dog's tooth.
It seems his sleeps were hind'red by thy railing,
And thereof comes it that his head is light. (69–72)

The abbess performs her Christian duty to protect Antipholus, taken in sanctuary in her priory, ending her speech with neatly symmetrical couplets: "The consequence is, then, thy jealous fits / Hath scared thy husband from the use of wits" (85–86). She promises to bring Antipholus to his wits again through the approved methods of her spiritual calling:

With wholesome syrups, drugs, and holy prayers,
To make of him a formal [sane, normal] man again.
It is a branch and parcel [part] of mine oath,
A charitable duty of my order. (104–7)

Antipholus, of course, is not mad. At the end of the play both the twins appear together and all confusion is cleared up. Happily—as in the proverbial happy ending—it turns out that Emilia is Egeon's long-lost wife. She entreats him to acknowledge the fortunate reality of the present moment:

> Speak, old Egeon, if thou beest the man
> That hadst a wife once called Emilia,
> That bore thee at a burden two fair sons! (342–44)

The play ends with the joyful resolution of all seeming inconsistencies. The abbess turns out to be the bearer of unexpected good tidings for all.

13. LUSTY OLDER WOMEN

Most of Shakespeare's lusty older women are lower class, which may explain their lively, colloquial style. The most obvious example is Dame Quickly, the hostess of the Eastcheap Tavern in *1* and *2 Henry IV,* who plays an important role in *The Merry Wives of Windsor* and also appears briefly in *Henry V.* We never find out how old she is, but in *2 Henry IV* she says that she has known Falstaff "twenty-nine years, come peascod-time" (2.4.392), or early summer. That would make her a contemporary of Falstaff in her late fifties or early sixties. In the same play Falstaff's page addresses her as "old Mistress Quickly" (2.2.151).

She is a passionate admirer of Falstaff. In *1 Henry IV,* when Falstaff plays the king, Dame Quickly is beside herself with astonishment. She says: "O Jesu, this is excellent sport, i' faith!" (2.4.390), to which Falstaff replies in character: "Weep not, sweet queen, for trickling tears are vain" (391). There is an obvious pun on "queen" as a noble and "quean" as a loose woman or prostitute. Dame Quickly is impressed with Falstaff's histrionic ability: "O, the Father, how he holds his countenance!" (392), meaning how he maintains the demeanor of his role. Falstaff continues in his mock-tragic style: "For God's sake, lords, convey my tristful [sorrowful] queen! / For tears do stop the floodgates of her eyes" (393–94). They are obviously playing to each other in a long and familiar relationship, and Dame Quickly is ecstatic: "O Jesu, he doth it as like one of these harlotry players as ever I see!" (395–96). "Harlotry"—meaning like a harlot, worthless and trashy—is here used as an admiring adjective by Dame Quickly, who is very lively and inventive in her diction.

She is particularly strong in invective. We have the impression that she is illiterate and distinguishes words mainly by their sounds. When she tells Prince Hal that Falstaff said he would cudgel him, Falstaff becomes abusive: "Go, you thing, go!" (3.3.118). "Thing" has negative sexual connotations, and the hostess is angry: "Say, what thing, what thing?" (119). Falstaff tries to worm out of any improper sense of "thing" when he replies: "What thing? Why, a thing to thank God on" (120). But the hostess is not appeased: "I am no thing to thank God on, I would thou shouldst know it! I am an honest man's wife, and, setting thy knighthood aside, thou art a knave to call me so" (121–24). She is beside herself when Falstaff calls her an otter: "Why, she's neither fish nor flesh; a man knows not where to have her" (130–31). Dame Quickly's answer multiplies bawdy suggestions: "Thou art an unjust man in saying so. Thou or any man knows where to have me, thou knave, thou!" (132–34). Dame Quickly seems entrapped in language, but she is keen on emotive connotations.

There is an earlier exchange in this scene when Falstaff accuses her of having stolen his valuable ring while he was sleeping: "Go to, you are a woman, go!" (63). The hostess is outraged: "Who, I? No; I defy thee! God's light, I was never called so in mine own house before!" (64–65). Dame Quickly seems to be thinking of "woman" as a term of opprobrium, as in "loose woman." Falstaff claims: "Go to, I know you well enough" (66), but Dame Quickly strongly objects: "No, Sir John; you do not know me, Sir John. I know you, Sir John. You owe me money, Sir John, and now you pick a quarrel to beguile me of it" (67–69). She may be illiterate, but she is shrewd and her speech is easy and energetic.

In *2 Henry IV* she takes legal action against Falstaff to recover the money he has filched from her. When Falstaff says: "Throw the quean [a loose woman, a harlot] in the channel [gutter]" (2.1.47–48), the hostess replies angrily: "Ah, thou honeysuckle villain! Wilt thou kill God's officers and the King's? Ah, thou honeyseed rogue! Thou art a honeyseed, a man-queller [man killer], and a woman-queller" (51–54). "Honeysuckle" and "honeyseed" are Dame Quickly's coinages for "homicidal," presumably a fancy legal term not in her everyday lexicon.

When she speaks with the chief justice, she has an extraordinary accumulation of irrelevant details that reminds us of Dogberry, the constable in *Much Ado About Nothing*, and Elbow, the constable in *Measure for Measure*. Her claim that Falstaff promised to marry her is accompanied by specifications that seek to locate the exact moment when he made his promise:

> Thou didst swear to me upon a parcel-gilt [partly gilded] goblet, sitting in my Dolphin chamber, at the round table, by a sea-coal fire, upon Wednesday in Wheeson [Whitsun] week, when the Prince broke thy head for liking [likening] his father to a singing-man of Windsor, thou didst swear to me then, as I was washing thy wound, to marry me and make me my lady thy wife. Canst thou deny it? Did not goodwife Keech, the butcher's wife, come in then and call me gossip Quickly? Coming in to borrow a mess of vinegar, telling us she had a good dish of prawns, whereby thou didst desire to eat some, whereby I told thee they were ill for a green [raw] wound? (87–100)

I have quoted this passage at length to indicate the randomness and free association typical of Dame Quickly's inimitable discourse.

In her tussle with Pistol, Falstaff's "ancient," or ensign, whom she wants to thrust down the stairs because he is a swaggerer, or blusterer, Dame Quickly speaks with particular ease in her own, partly invented language. She calls him "Captain Pizzle," or penis (especially of an animal such as a bull), phonetically punning on his name: "Good Captain Pizzle, be quiet. 'Tis very late, i' faith. I beseek you now, aggravate [moderate] your choler" (165–66). It is unclear whether "beseek" is a northern provincialism for "beseech" or if Dame Quickly is speaking in her invented language. Pistol answers in his own flamboyant, allusive, and garbled style:

> Shall packhorses
> And hollow pampered jades of Asia,
> Which cannot go but thirty mile a day,
> Compare with Caesar, and with Cannibals,
> And Trojan Greeks? (167–71)

Dame Quickly is dumbfounded by Pistol's discourse and says only: "By my troth, Captain, these are very bitter words" (174–75). Why "bitter"? This is one of those puzzling but memorable lines in Shakespeare. Clearly she doesn't understand a word of Pistol's rant and interprets it in her own illiterate fashion. Pistol is definitely a swaggerer in his discourse but never in his actions. That is enough, however, for both Dame Quickly and Doll Tearsheet, an available woman in the tavern in Eastcheap, to want to get rid of him.

Mistress Quickly plays a somewhat different role in *The Merry Wives of Windsor*. She is a servant of Doctor Caius, the French physician, but she is also a general messenger and go-between. Falstaff calls her "my good she-Mercury" (2.2.79–80), who is also known as Hermes, the messenger of the gods. She speaks endless malapropisms, as in the *Henry IV* plays, usually with a sexual double entendre. For example, when Falstaff complains that he was thrown into a laundry basket to escape from the premises of Mistress Ford, Mistress Quickly explains: "Alas the day, good heart, that was not her fault. She does so take on with her men; they mistook their erection" (3.5.38–40). Here "erection" was substituted for "direction," or what they were directed to do. Falstaff picks up the bawdy connotation: "So did I mine, to build upon a foolish woman's promise" (41–42).

The language games are most obvious in act 4, scene 1, where Parson Evans, a Welshman, instructs William, a son of the Pages, in Latin grammar. This is an amusing set piece that has nothing to do with the plot of the play. Everything stops while Mistress Quickly delivers her unintentionally bawdy comments on Latin grammar, which come directly out of the pages of William Lilly's textbook, first published in 1549 and widely used in grammar schools. When Evans asks, in his stage-Welsh accent, "What is the focative case, William?," William replies, "O—*vocativo*, O." Evans cautions: "Remember, William; focative is *caret*." Dame Quickly can't believe what she is hearing and says only: "And that's a good root" (48–52). For Evans's "focative" she obviously hears "fuckative." Carrot and root also have phallic connotations.

But when Evans asks about the genitive case, Mistress Quickly cannot contain her indignation. William says "Genitive—*horum, harum, horum*," which Mistress Quickly interprets phonetically not as Latin but as English: "Vengeance of Jenny's case! Fie on her! Never name her, child, if she be a whore" (58–60). "Case" is a slang word for the female genitalia. Mistress Quickly's anger knows no bounds and she remonstrates against Parson Evans: "You do ill to teach the child such words. He teaches him to hick and hack, which they'll do fast enough of themselves, and to call 'horum.' Fie upon you!" (62–65). Poor Parson Evans's Welsh accent catches him up in a very bawdy scene, like the language lesson in *Henry V* (3.4). It is not clear what "hick and hack" mean, but it is definitely something sexual.

The Nurse in *Romeo and Juliet* is a lot like Mistress Quickly. She is definitely lower class and old. Early in the play she informs us that she has only four teeth left (1.3.13). Both her daughter, Susan, and her husband are dead. She was a wet nurse for Juliet, who is now almost fourteen. Like Pandarus in *Troilus and Cressida*, she subsequently complains to Juliet of her "aching bones" (2.5.64), but in her case it clearly means that she is tired. It is a pleasure to hear her object to the bawdy Mercutio, who exits with the phrase "Farewell, ancient lady" (2.4.150). Like Mistress Quickly's displeasure with Pistol in *2 Henry IV*, the Nurse is indignant over Mercutio's disrespectful style. He calls her "a bawd, a bawd, a bawd! So ho!" (136). "So ho" is a hunter's cry when he has found his prey. The Nurse complains to Romeo: "And [if] 'a speak anything against me, I'll take him down, and 'a were lustier than he is, and twenty such Jacks; and if I cannot, I'll find those that shall. Scurvy knave! I am none of his flirt-gills; I am none of his skainsmates"(157–61). The meaning of "skains-mates" is unclear, but "skain" refers to a long Irish knife. The Nurse speaks with great slangy vigor. She is not overtly sexual, but everything she says seems to have a double meaning, as in "take him down."

Like Mistress Quickly, the Nurse is rambling and garrulous in her discourse. It takes her an awfully long time to give Romeo Juliet's message:

> Pray you, sir, a word; and, as I told you, my young lady bid me
> inquire you out. What she bid me say, I will keep to myself; but
> first let me tell ye, if ye should lead her in a fool's paradise, as they
> say, it were a very gross kind of behavior, as they say. (169–74)

"As they say" seems to lend authority to the Nurse's speech. She doesn't immediately grasp Romeo's answer, which she confuses with Romeo's initial comment "I protest unto thee—" (179), which he never finishes. The Nurse's conclusion is: "I will tell her, sir, that you do protest, which, as I take it, is a gentlemanlike offer" (184–85). The Nurse's report to Juliet of what Romeo has said is equally roundabout: "Your love says, like an honest gentleman, and a courteous, and a kind, and a handsome, and, I warrant, a virtuous—Where is your mother?" (2.5.56–58). Juliet cannot believe that her true love's message is "Where is your mother?," but through the windings and twistings of the Nurse's garrulous report the true message finally emerges.

When Juliet, who is secretly married to the banished Romeo, refuses to marry Paris, her father unleashes his wrath against her. At the end of the scene Juliet is alone with the Nurse, whom she begs for comfort. The Nurse is practical, like Emilia toward Desdemona in *Othello* (4.3), and advises Juliet to make the most of her present situation:

> I think it best you married with the County [Paris].
> O, he's a lovely gentleman!
> Romeo's a dishclout to him. An eagle, madam,
> Hath not so green, so quick, so fair an eye
> As Paris hath. (3.5.219–23)

Why is Romeo only a "dishclout"? The Nurse wants to make the best of things as they now stand, but when she leaves Juliet is horrified:

Ancient damnation! O most wicked fiend!
Is it more sin to wish me thus forsworn,
Or to dispraise my lord with that same tongue
Which she hath praised him with above compare
So many thousand times? (237–41)

"Ancient damnation" is strong language, but Juliet now needs to separate herself from her Nurse as well as her mother and father, all of whom have abandoned her. The Nurse undoubtedly means well, but she is definitely not a moral creature.

The Nurse is overcome with grief when she finds Juliet's lifeless body in her bed on her marriage day, but her speech is intertwined with suggestive slang and many double entendres:

The County Paris hath set up his rest [resolved]
That you shall rest but little. God forgive me!
Marry, and amen. (4.5.6–8)

Although the Nurse is aware of the bawdy implications of what she is saying and asks for forgiveness, she continues in exactly the same vein: "Ay, let the County take you in your bed; / He'll fright you up, i' faith. Will it not be?" (10–11). When she finds Juliet lifeless, she grieves: "O weraday [welladay] that ever I was born! / Some *aqua vitae*, ho!" (15–16). Like Dame Quickly, in her misfortune she immediately calls for strong drink.

Tamora in *Titus Andronicus* is a very different figure from either the Nurse or Dame Quickly. She is not lower class and doesn't speak in the salty slang of those characters. She describes herself as a "lascivious Goth" (2.3.110) and is in love with Aaron the Moor, another of Titus's captives. There is no specific indication of her age, but she has three grown sons: Alarbus, Chiron, and Demetrius. When she marries Saturninus, she speaks as if she is much older than he is:

If Saturnine advance the Queen of Goths,
She will a handmaid be to his desires,
A loving nurse, a mother to his youth. (1.1.331–33)

Shakespeare doesn't explain in what ways she is "a mother to his youth," but she is his constant adviser and counselor. For example, she tells him how to deal with Titus: "My lord, be ruled by me, be won at last, / Dissemble all your griefs and discontents" (443–44). She is bent on revenge from the very beginning of the play because Titus has allowed her son Alarbus to be sacrificed: "I'll find a day to massacre them all, / And race [raze] their faction and their family" (451–52). She will let them know "what 'tis to let a queen / Kneel in the streets and beg for grace in vain" (455–56).

Tamora has a very convincing sex scene with Aaron when they are alone together in the woods. Shakespeare takes as his model the scene between Dido and Aeneas in Virgil's *Aeneid*:

We may, each wreathèd in the other's arms,
(Our pastimes done) possess a golden slumber,
Whiles hounds and horns and sweet melodious birds
Be unto us as is a nurse's song
Of lullaby to bring her babe asleep. (2.3.25–29)

It is a very literary, pastoral scene, but Aaron demurs:

Madam, though Venus govern your desires,
Saturn is dominator over mine. (30–31)

Saturn is the god of melancholy, and Aaron is firmly committed to vengeance. Yet even though she is thwarted in her desires, Tamora still says: "Ah, my sweet Moor, sweeter to me than life!" (51).

Tamora is proud of her rhetorical skills and her ability to outwit everyone, as she reveals in an aside: "Why, thus it shall become / High-witted Tamora to gloze [deceive in speech] with all" (4.4.34–35).

However, when she appears to Titus as Revenge and her two sons as Rape and Murder, Titus easily outwits her. As he says to her directly: "I am not mad, I know thee well enough" (5.2.21). Tamora doesn't believe him and tells her sons:

> Whate'er I forge to feed his brainsick humors,
> Do you uphold and maintain in your speeches,
> For now he firmly takes me for Revenge,
> And, being credulous in this mad thought,
> I'll make him send for Lucius his son. (71–75)

Tamora's sons end badly. As Titus gloats:

> Why, there they are, both bakèd in this pie,
> Whereof their mother daintily hath fed,
> Eating the flesh that she herself hath bred. (5.3.60–62)

He then stabs Tamora and is immediately stabbed by Saturninus.

It is tempting to add Venus, from the poem *Venus and Adonis,* to this list of lustful older women, but her age is never specified. In fact, she is a goddess and ageless. But there is a conflict between her godlike qualities and her very human lustfulness as she pursues the young, virginal Adonis. Venus doesn't sound like an immortal at several points in the poem, such as: "By this the lovesick queen began to sweat" (175). *Venus and Adonis* is an erotic verse epyllion, like Marlowe's *Hero and Leander,* and its aim is to titillate its audience. The contrast between the immortal goddess and the sweating, middle-aged woman is intended to tease the reader. Venus asks Adonis how he can possibly resist her charms since she is perfect:

> Were I hard-favored, foul [ugly], or wrinkled old,
> Ill-nurtured, crooked, churlish, harsh in voice,
> O'erworn, despisèd, rheumatic, and cold,
> Thick-sighted, barren, lean, and lacking juice,

Then mightst thou pause, for then I were not for thee;
But having no defects, why dost abhor me? (133–38)

Venus unwittingly presents a catalogue of all the defects of old age in a woman, but she doesn't act like a young ingénue in the poem. She pursues Adonis relentlessly not in order to make him fall in love with her, but only to enjoy him sexually.

CONCLUSION

Shakespeare was born in 1564 and died in 1616 at the age of fifty-two. As far as one can tell, this was a normal life span in the early seventeenth century. Perhaps one could stretch this a few years to a life expectancy of fifty-five or sixty—but not much more. The point of these calculations is to determine what effect Shakespeare's own life had on his ideas about aging. If Shakespeare retired from the theater around 1608, or reduced his active participation in the affairs of the King's Men, his company of actors, he was only in his mid-forties. Furthermore, the *Sonnets*, which were probably written in the 1590s when Shakespeare was in his early thirties, speak of the poet—in contrast to the young man to whom the sonnets were addressed—as an old and withered person. There is obviously a bit a poetic license involved here, but Sonnet 2 begins with the beautiful young man transformed and facing an unpredictable future: "When forty winters shall besiege thy brow." His "youth's proud livery" will become "a tottered weed [tattered garment] of small worth held."

It is difficult to reach any firm conclusions about the topic of aging in Shakespeare. As usual, Shakespeare wants to have it both ways, both positive and negative, as if this posture is necessary to promote the sense of dramatic conflict. King Lear is a good case in point. He is clearly foolish in proposing the love test. He is petulant and impulsive in rejecting those who love him most, like Cordelia and Kent. He is trying to do the impossible, namely, to abdicate yet retain the title and all the appurtenances of a king. He wants the unloving Goneril and Regan to take care of him and his hundred knights as if he were a young, wayward child. The first scene of the play unleashes tremendous tragic potentialities, with Lear seeming to bring his ruin upon himself. Regan may be ill-willed, but she is shrewd in her judgment that her father "hath ever but slenderly known himself" (1.1.294–95). Lear gradually realizes that he has taken "too little care" of the "poor naked wretches" (3.4.33, 28) that are an essential part of his kingdom. When he recovers from his madness, he realizes something about his common humanity: "I am a very foolish, fond old man, / Fourscore and upward, not an hour more nor less" (4.7.60–61). This is a very different Lear from the one we encountered in the first scene of the play. His painful awareness that he is an old man is a significant part of his tragic recognition.

Although there is a good deal of gerontological knowledge and speculation about what it was like to be old in the late sixteenth and early seventeenth centuries, there is a marked difference between data about aging and the sense of aging in Shakespeare's works. It is clear that Shakespeare uses familiar imagery to reflect the ravages of time, with Time depicted with the traditional hourglass and scythe—a figure still encountered on New Year's cards. This imagery is most obviously employed in the *Sonnets,* but it runs throughout Shakespeare's works in his representation of mutability, a strongly biblical theme. White hair and wrinkles are part of the oft-repeated iconography of aging. The physical infirmities of old age are all laid out in conventional images very similar to the representation of old age in the twenty-first century. Yet there is an abiding sense that old age also brings with it a degree of wisdom gained through a long and serious confrontation with life experience. Before he dies King Henry IV gains a new understanding of "the revolution of the times" (*2 Henry IV*, 3.1.46). Even the complaining and often tedious Queen Margaret in the *Henry VI* plays and *Richard III* serves as a spokesperson of conscience and memory.

It may seem disappointing that Shakespeare refuses to grapple with the ideological implications of old age. There is no ultimate reconciliation of different and contradictory representations. Critics are tempted to read the plays in relation to Shakespeare's life—or to his life pleasantly fictionalized by reference to his writing. This is a great temptation for biographers, who remain frustrated by the lack of specific facts. Of course, this isn't entirely misguided since there is usually some unstated relation between a writer's life and his works. One could reverse this and claim that a writer projects fictional selves and personalities into his works. How can one explain the nefarious fact that Shakespeare is so accomplished in his portrayal of villains, that Iago should be so much more compellingly written than Othello? A gross example of this fallacy of reading Shakespeare's fictions as biographical fact is the claim that since *Timon of Athens* expounds so knowledgeably about syphilis, Shakespeare must have been suffering from a veneral disease when he wrote the play. One thing, however, is certain. The fact that aging is such a significant theme in Shakespeare is proof of his own anxieties about growing old.

NOTES

INTRODUCTION

1. All quotations from Shakespeare refer to the individual volumes of *The Complete Signet Classic Shakespeare*, ed. Sylvan Barnet (New York: Harcourt Brace Jovanovich, 1972), with the exception of *King Lear,* in the Arden edition, 3rd ser., ed. R. A. Foakes (London: Thomson Learning, 1997).

2. For abundant literature on this theme see: Samuel C. Chew, "This Strange Eventful History," in *Joseph Quincy Adams Memorial Studies*, ed. J. G. McManaway et al. (Washington, D.C.: Folger Library, 1948), 157–82; Elizabeth Sears, *The Ages of Man* (Princeton, N.J.: Princeton University Press, 1986); J. A. Burrow, *The Ages of Man* (Oxford: Clarendon Press, 1986); Hanna Scolnicov, "Ages of Man, Ages of Woman," *Cahiers Elisabéthains* 57 (2000): 61–78; and William Jeffrey Phelan, "The Vale of Years: Early Modern Aging, Gender, and Shakespearean Tragedy" (Ph.D. diss., University of California, Los Angeles, 1997), ch. 2. Available online at ProQuest.

3. See John Wilders, *Antony and Cleopatra*, Arden ed., 3rd ser. (London: Thomson Learning, 1995).

4. See Keith Thomas, "Age and Authority in Early Modern England," *Proceedings of the British Academy* 62 (1976): 205–48; Steven R. Smith, "Death, Dying, and the Elderly in Seventeenth Century England," in *Aging and the Elderly*, ed. Stuart F. Spicker et al. (Atlantic Highlands, N.J.: Humanities Press, 1978), 205–19; E. A. Wrigley and R. S. Schofield, *The Population History of England 1541–1871: A Reconstruction* (Cambridge, Mass.: Harvard University Press, 1981); *Aging in the Past*, ed. David I. Kent and Peter Laslett (Berkeley: University of California Press, 1995); E. A. Wrigley et al., *English Population History from Family Reconstitution, 1580–1837* (Cambridge: Cambridge University Press, 1997); and Lynn A. Botelho, "The 17th Century," in *A History of Old Age*, ed. Pat Thane (Los Angeles, Calif.: Getty Museum, 2005), 113–74.

5. Peter Laslett, "Necessary Knowledge: Age and Aging in the Societies of the Past," in *Aging in the Past*, 19.

6. Lawrence Stone, *The Family, Sex and Marriage in England, 1500–1800*, abridged ed. (New York: Harper, 1979), graph 5.

7. See Sara Mendelson and Patricia Crawford, *Women in Early Modern England 1550–1720* (Oxford: Clarendon Press, l998); *Women and Ageing in British Society Since 1500*, ed. Lynn Botelho and Pat Thane (Harlow, Eng., 2001); see also Aki C. L. Beam, "'Should I as Yet Call You Old?': Testing the Boundaries of Female Old Age in Early Modern England," in *Growing Old in Early Modern Europe: Cultural Representations*, ed. Erin Campbell (Burlington, Vt.: Ashgate, 2006), 95–116.

8. The studies by Jeanne Addison Roberts are relevant here: "Types of Crone: The Nurse and the Wise Woman in English Renaissance Drama," in *Renaissance Papers 2000* [Southeastern Renaissance Conference], vol. 47, ed. T. H. Howard-Hill and Philip Rollinson (Rochester, N.Y.: Boydell & Brewer, 2000), 71–86; and "The Crone in English Renaissance Drama," *Medieval and Renaissance Drama in England* 15 (2003): 116–37.

9. Phelan's dissertation ("The Vale of Years: Early Modern Aging, Gender, and Shakespearean Tragedy," esp. chap. 1) is undoubtedly the best single book on the subject of aging in Shakespeare. See also Steven R. Smith, "Growing Old in Early Stuart England," *Albion* 8 (1976): 125–41.

On the general topic of Shakespeare and old age, see the comprehensive essay by Thomas M. Cranfill, "Flesh's Thousand Natural Shocks in Shakespeare," *Texas Studies in Literature and Language* 17 (1975): 27–60; Ernest H. Cox, "Shakespeare and Some Conventions of Old Age," *Studies in Philology* 39 (1942): 36–46; and Hallett Smith, "'Bare Ruined Choirs': Shakespearean Variations on the Theme of Old Age," *Huntington Library Quarterly* 39 (1976): 233–49. See also L. Wardlaw Miles, "Shakespeare's Old Men," *ELH* 7 (1940): 286–99; John W. Draper, "Shakespeare's Attitude Towards Old Age," *Journal of Gerontology* 1 (1946): 118–26; Herbert S. Donow, "'To Everything There Is a Season': Some Shakespearean Models of Normal and Anomalous Aging," *The Gerontologist* 32 (1992): 733–38; and Bruce Wayne Coggin, "Studies in Shakespeare's Treatment of Old Age" (Ph.D. diss., University of Texas at Austin, 1982).

1. *KING LEAR, TITUS ANDRONICUS,* AND *CYMBELINE*

1. See William Jeffrey Phelan, "The Vale of Years: Early Modern Aging, Gender, and Shakespearean Tragedy" (Ph.D. diss., University of California, Los Angeles, 1997), chap. 5; Susan Snyder, "*King Lear* and the Psychology of Dying," *Shakespeare Quarterly* 33 (1982): 449–60; and Carolyn Asp, "'The Clamor of Errors': Freud, Aging, and *King Lear,*" in *Memory and Desire: Aging in Literature–Psychoanalysis,* ed. Kathleen Woodward and Murray M. Schwartz (Bloomington: Indiana University Press, 1986), 192–204. See also John W. Draper, "The Old Age of King Lear," *Journal of English and Germanic Philology* 39 (1940): 527–40; H. A. Mason, "Can We Derive Wisdom about Old Age from *King Lear*?," *Cambridge Quarterly* 6 (1975): 203–13; Marion D. Perret, "*Lear's* Good Old Man," *Shakespeare Studies* 17 (1985): 89–102; Coppélia Kahn, "The Absent Mother in *King Lear,*" in *Rewriting the Renaissance*, ed. Margaret W. Ferguson (Chicago: University of Chicago Press, 1986), 33–49; Arthur Kirsch, "The Emotional Landscape of King Lear," *Shakespeare Quarterly* 39 (1988): 154–70; David Bevington, "'Is this the Promised End?': Death and Dying in *King Lear,*" *Proceedings of the American Philosophical Society* 133 (1989): 404–15; Janet Adelman, *Suffocating Mothers* (New York: Routledge, 1992); and Nina Taunton, *Fictions of Old Age in Early Modern Literature and Culture* (London: Routledge, 2007).

2. R. A. Foakes, introduction to *King Lear,* Arden ed., 3rd ser., ed. R. A. Foakes (London: Thomson Learning, 1997). See also R. A. Foakes, "King Lear: Monarch or Senior Citizen?," in *Essays in Honor of S. Schoenbaum,* ed. R. B. Parker and S. P. Zitner (Newark: University of Delaware Press, 1996), 271–89.

3. See my article "Hamlet's O-groans and Textual Criticism," *Renaissance Drama,* n.s., 9 (1978) : 109–19.

4. The relationship between the two plays is developed in my discussion of *Titus Andronicus* in the Harvester New Critical Introductions to Shakespeare, ed. Graham Bradshaw (Hemel Hempstead, Eng.: Harvester Wheatsheaf, 1990).

2. THE AGING PROCESS, WITH SPECIAL REFERENCE TO *MACBETH*

1. See Mable Buland, *The Presentation of Time in the Elizabethan Drama*, Yale Studies in English no. 44 (New Haven, Conn.: Yale University Press, 1912).

3. TIME THE DESTROYER IN THE *SONNETS* AND *THE RAPE OF LUCRECE*

1. Katherine Duncan-Jones, ed., *Shakespeare's Sonnets,* Arden ed., 3rd ser. (London: Thomson Learning, 1997).

4. "HEAVY" FATHERS

1. See the following: David G. Brailow, "Prospero's 'Old Brain': The Old Man as Metaphor in *The Tempest,*" *Shakespeare Studies* 14 (1981): 285–303; Sara Munson Deats, "The Dialectic of Aging in Shakespeare's *King Lear* and *The Tempest,*" in *Aging and Identity: A Humanities Perspective,* ed. Sara Munson Deats and Lagretta Tallent Lenker (Westport, Conn.: Praeger, 1990), 23–32; and Philip D. Collington, "Sans Wife: Sexual Anxiety and the Old Man in Shakespeare," in *Growing Old in Early Modern Europe,* ed. Erin Campbell (Burlington, Vt.: Ashgate, 2006), 185–207.

5. POLITIC OLD MEN: POLONIUS, NESTOR, AND MENENIUS

1. See Nina Taunton, "Time's Whirligig: Images of Old Age in *Coriolanus,* Francis Bacon and Thomas Newton," in *Growing Old in Early Modern Europe,* ed. Erin Campbell (Burlington, Vt.: Ashgate, 2006), 21–38; and

Nina Taunton, *Fictions of Old Age in Early Modern Literature and Culture* (London: Routledge, 2007), esp. chap. 5.

6. WISE OLD MEN

1. See Steven Marx, "'Fortunate Senex': The Pastoral of Old Age," *Studies in English Literature* 25 (1985): 21–44.

7. FALSTAFF

1. See Ruth E. Sims, "The Green Old Age of Falstaff," *Bulletin of the History of Medicine* 13 (1943): 144–57. On *puer senex* see Edgar Wind, "Ripeness Is All," in *Pagan Mysteries in the Renaissance* (New Haven, Conn.: Yale University Press, 1958), 97–112.

2. Quoted from the introduction to the Arden edition of *The Merry Wives of Windsor*, ed. H. J. Oliver (London: Methuen, 1971), xliv–xlv.

8. JEALOUS OLD MEN: OTHELLO AND LEONTES

1. See Phelan diss., chap. 3; Edward A. Snow, "Sexual Anxiety and the Male Order of Things in *Othello*," *English Literary Renaissance* 10 (1980): 384–412; Janet C. Stavropoulos, "Love and Age in *Othello*," *Shakespeare Studies* 19 (1987): 125–41; and Valerie Barnes Lipscomb, "'Yet That's Not Much': Age Differences in *Othello*," *Journal of Aging and Identity* 6 (2001): 209–21.

2. See the Arden edition of *The Winter's Tale*, ed. J. H. P. Pafford (London: Methuen, 1963).

3. John Donne, "The Autumnal," in *The Elegies* and *The Songs and Sonnets*, ed. Helen Gardner (Oxford: Clarendon Press, 1965), 27.

9. OLD WARRIORS AND STATESMEN IN THE ENGLISH HISTORY PLAYS

1. See Thomas M. Cranfill, "Shakespeare's Old Heroes," *Texas Studies in Literature and Language* 15 (1973): 215–30.

10. FATAL ATTRACTION: *ANTONY AND CLEOPATRA*

1. John Wilders, Arden edition of *Antony and Cleopatra*, 3rd ser. (London: Thomson Learning, 1995). See also Phelan diss., chap. 4.

2. See Wilders, Arden edition of *Antony and Cleopatra,* 255.

11. POWERFUL OLDER WOMEN

1. See Nina Taunton, "Time's Whirligig: Images of Old Age in *Coriolanus*, Francis Bacon and Thomas Newton," in *Growing Old in Early Modern Europe*, ed. Campbell, 21–38.

2. See Jean E. Howard and Phyllis Rackin, *Engendering a Nation* (London: Routledge, 1997), 83–99.

3. Quoted in the Arden edition of *King Henry VI, Part III*, ed. Andrew S. Cairncross (London: Metheun, 1964), xli.

4. See Richard Levin, "Gertrude's Elusive Libido and Shakespeare's Unreliable Narrators," *Studies in English Literature* 48 (2008): 305–26.

INDEX

Venus and Adonis, 10, 101, 107, 161–62

Virgil's *Aeneid*, 70, 72, 160

Volumnia, 9, 73, 75–76, 127–31, 141

Werblud-Moore, Elaine, v

Wilders, John, 119–20, 168, 172

Wind, Edgar, 171

Winter's Tale, The, 5, 8, 10, 32, 36, 78, 98, 103–8, 145–48

Wolsey, Cardinal, 8–9, 112, 115–18, 148–49

Wrigley, E. A., 168

York, Duchess of, 134–36